Developing a Forest School in Early Years Provision

A practical han...   ...in any early years setting

...lchem

Conten...

Published by Practical Pre-School Books,
A Division of MA Education Ltd, St Jude's Church,
Dulwich Road, Herne Hill, London, SE24 0PB.

Tel: 020 7738 5454

www.practicalpreschoolbooks.com

© MA Education Ltd 2012.

All images © MA Education Ltd.

Front cover images: main image photo taken by Katherine Milchem,
bottom row: photos taken by Lucie Carlier and Jenny Doyle.

ISBN 978-1-907241-34-5

Introduction

This book is a practical guide for practitioners who know little about Forest School and wish to know more or those who are thinking of starting down the exciting road of developing Forest School for themselves and their setting. The book draws on first-hand experience of the authors as well as case studies and working examples of good practice.

It starts by looking at the roots of Forest School and its place in relation to history, early years education and theorists and the more recent import of the ethos and philosophy from Scandinavia. It discusses why and how Forest School became established in the United Kingdom.

Following this, the book covers the first steps and training needed when embarking down the Forest School route, as well as looking at options and examples of where Forest School is successfully run: essential and optional features, insurance and landowner agreements.

There is an informative section on organising, planning, evaluating and documenting the sessions, with case studies from settings. The balance between child-initiated learning and adult-led experiences in supporting and scaffolding children's ideas at Forest School is discussed alongside continuing the learning journey back in the setting or home environment.

A diverse range of experiences may take place at Forest School. This title focuses on how to maximise on the ever-changing landscape, seasons, weather, flora and fauna offered by the natural environment and the opportunities for storytelling and storymaking.

The role of the adult and the leader's communication with the wider community is also addressed, including: parents, carers, family members, child-minders, volunteers, senior management, Ofsted inspectors, local government officers, landowners, foresters or rangers.

A Forest School environment can nurture cultural diversity and make everyone feel valued, using the knowledge and expertise each can bring to the experience. The book covers this and how Forest School can be just as much an alien environment for adults as well as children.

The book concludes with expressing where Forest Schools stand now in the UK and what the future may hold; in the ever-changing world of local government and how the new Forest School Association is aiming to take Forest School forward.

Chapter 1:
What is Forest School?

Forest School – two words that over the last fifteen years seem to have captured the imagination of early years practitioners and other educators all over the United Kingdom (UK). Much has been written about Forest School in various guises, but why has this form of learning become one of the fastest growing movements in education – probably more than any other initiative in recent times? And why not driven from government but from grass roots: the practitioners? Questions frequently asked are: "What is 'Forest School'? Do I need a woodland?". Before questions like these can be answered, we need to explore why and where this form of learning originated.

Forest School in the UK can be traced back to 1930s when educators from the Woodcraft Folk, Quakers and the Order of Woodcraft Chivalry started promoting the 'Woodcraft Way', a movement started in the early 1990s in America by Ernest Thompson Seton. The influence for this movement came from the beliefs and lifestyle of Native Americans and how they lived with and close to nature. In 1948 residential camps began with the aspiration to pass on the ways and values of these native people through living outdoors and essentially community participation. It was the practical, hands on, positive and creative experiences that were felt necessary to appreciate nature that became the philosophy of the camps. Living 'in tune' with nature was seen to kindle an inner feeling of well-being and contentment. At camp, children are taught to care for themselves, each other and the environment: a sentiment reiterated in the recently published 'Sustainable Schools' framework (DCSF 2008). The society that became Forest School Camps still arrange weekend and holiday camps for young people.

More recently, what is now in education and environmental circles commonly known as Forest School, has been adapted from the Scandinavian approach to early years provision. In Scandinavian countries, just as in the UK, there is a variety of provision for children in the pre-school years. However, being outdoors and close to nature is much more embedded in Scandinavian culture and this is reflected in their pre-school provision. In Denmark you find the 'Naturbornhaven' and 'Skogsbornehaven'. 'Bornehaven' meaning kindergarten (German translation for children's garden), 'skog' meaning wood or forest and 'natur' is obviously nature. In Norway and Sweden they have 'Friluftsliv', meaning open-air living, as part of the curriculum. In these countries the children have 'Smogsmulle' who is a mythical friend who teaches the children about nature throughout the year. Finland has a similar character called 'Mettsamori'. The stories around these creatures and their friends reflect the seasons and rhythm of the year, in a similar way to Forest School camps reflecting life of the Native Americans. The philosophy is based on the desire to provide young children with an education that encourages an appreciation of the wide, natural world and which would encourage responsibility for nature conservation in later life.

First Forest School in the UK

It was Bridgwater College in Somerset, following a visit by students to Denmark in 1993, who started this recent form of Forest School in the UK. In Denmark, the college students observed young children being escorted into woodland and allowed free exploration of the outdoor spaces. The children were confident and learned to appreciate the natural environment about them. Activities were not set; it was the environment that afforded the rich learning experience. The children were capable and competent learners and were encouraged to use tools, grow and pick vegetables and cook over a campfire.

The students and the tutors who accompanied them were so impressed and inspired by the Danish settings and their use of the outdoor environment, they decided to incorporate a similar way of working with children attending the college crèche. Importing a totally different culture and ethos was impractical – so they started short sessions on the college playing field. Here they observed their children's curiosity and imagination, watching thoughts scaffold and materials morphing continuously as the groups built upon ideas, skills and concepts. Children achieved because there were no expectations as to what the end result should look like. Practitioners gained a greater insight into the abilities and interests of the children, which led to a change in how the whole nursery environment was developed. These sessions grew to what we now call Forest School.

During that first year, the children grew in independence, confidence and self-esteem through the mastery of small achievable tasks and open-ended play. It was these qualities that the Bridgwater college students had witnessed in the Danish pre-schools, and was now evident in their own children who had been attending Forest School. A child is never set up to fail, each task is achievable, play is rich. So, in 1996 with the successful pilot behind them, Bridgwater College sourced areas of woodland, within a short minibus ride from the college, to continue and expand the Forest School sessions. All children attending the crèche, from the age of three, were given the opportunity to attend Forest School and students from the Additional Learning Needs area of the college also attended sessions in the woodland. Their pioneering work was beginning to be recognised in the wider education community and lead personnel from across the country started to visit Bridgwater to learn more about the Forest School approach.

A selection of training courses was developed to give educators, students, parent, carers, and volunteers the skills required to work in remote outdoor environment. These courses were validated by the awarding body Edexel (BTEC) and are discussed further in Chapter 2.

Bridgwater College was awarded the Queen's Anniversary Award for their pioneering work at Forest School and in 2000 they started to disseminate this practice and train practitioners from other local authorities.

What do we mean by Forest School?

In 2002, following the first national Forest School Conference, with support from the Forestry Commission and the Forest Education Initiative (FEI) Co-ordinator, a network was formed to assess national interest and map the growth of Forest School in the UK. The network defined Forest School as:

'An inspirational process that offers children, young people and adults regular opportunities to achieve, develop confidence and self-esteem through hands on learning experiences in a local woodland environment' (Forest School (England) Network 2002).

This definition is still widely used today although some regions have written their own.

A REFLECTION FROM AUTHOR JENNY DOYLE

In March 2000 I spent an inspiring week at Bishops Wood Centre in Worcestershire undertaking a Forest School Leadership Award. It was a beautiful setting and the tutors were inspirational.

We spent five days learning about recent brain development research, schemas, health and safety, woodland and management and practical skills. Much of what we were doing reminded me of my childhood and the sort of activities my brother and I enjoyed. Although I had grown up in Birmingham I mainly played in the local 'rec' (recreation ground) were we spent our time building dens, climbing trees and generally being creative with little or no equipment and most of all no adult supervision.

Driving home at the end of the week, I remember thinking 'but what do I actually do with the children in my care?'. I didn't have a woodland and I worked in a very urban environment. However we did have a space, albeit a very sterile tarmac school playground, but fortunately surrounded by a playing field. I had quite a challenging nursery group. Over 50% of the children were in the 'looked after sector' with a plethora of associated difficulties.

After talking to staff about what I had learned and receiving their support, I decided to take the children outside into the school grounds, without setting up the usual activities, and observe carefully their behaviour. There was a single tree on the grass next to the playground. The children congregated under this tree and began picking up sticks and leaves. One girl let her leaf blow in the wind and gradually several children joined in and they had leaf races across the playground. This spontaneous game, very different to any I had noticed before, was the start of our Forest School sessions. I ran six sessions on the school field before sourcing access to a woodland, about a twenty-minute minibus ride from school, where we visited for a further eight weeks until the end of term.

There was a noticeable change to each and every one of the children. One particularly quiet girl, who needed a lot of encouragement to try anything new in nursery, mastered crawling over a fallen log straddled across a stream and instigated a game of 'The Three Billy Goats Gruff'. This transferred back into the setting only using a balance beam as the log or 'bridge'.

Foxgloves provided an interesting discussion on their name. Did foxes really wear gloves? How many pairs would they need? The changing flora gave rise to lots of observation and conversation which seemed to flow much more naturally than indoors.

One boy, with particularly challenging behaviour, loved being given the responsibility of using a bow saw to cut logs for the fire. One morning he came into nursery and asked "if I be good today can I use your big sword?". (He meant 'saw' not 'sword' and wanted to use the bow saw). Each day we negotiated a goal. For example, if he didn't throw a chair or hit another child he was able to use the bow saw. He really started to think about the consequence of his behaviour and although he didn't always achieve his goal was very proud on the days he did.

Many settings however, without access to woodland, successfully run Forest School sessions in other areas including school grounds, local parks, wildlife areas, allotments and community gardens. The variety of areas will be further explored in Chapter 2. It is the philosophy and ethos, more than the area, that defines Forest School.

What makes a Forest School session different?

- Forest School is fun.

- The area: This is left as natural as possible. Logs or log slices are used to create a seating circle as a base, sometimes with a fire pit in the centre and possibly a semi-permanent shelter constructed as a space to store bags and equipment or refuge from very inclement weather.

- The children visit the area on a regular basis throughout the year; building upon their knowledge and familiarity of the area. They negotiate and learn to abide by standards of behaviour and respect each other and the environment.

- The children, within a regular routine, initiate their own learning. There may be focused activity, but this usually builds upon the children's interests from the previous session.

- The children learn to understand and manage risk.

- The adults: Forest School is led by qualified Level 3 leaders (See Chapter 2).

- There is a high adult:child ratio. These can be practitioners, students, parents, carers or volunteers.

- Observations of the children can often identify learning styles more easily in this environment–helping practitioners to plan for better children's learning in the setting.

To enable access to the outdoors in all weathers, if possible, supply waterproof clothing for both children and adults. The Scandinavians say: 'There is no such thing as bad weather, just poor clothing'. Unlike our Scandinavian neighbours, our modern lifestyles do not always include spending time outdoors in all types of weather and therefore we do not always have suitable clothing. Clothing should reflect not only the weather and season but also take into consideration the site and safety. On a warm summer day it can be several degrees cooler in a woodland beneath a dense canopy and sun hats may not be necessary, but in the local park natural shade may not be available and sun hats would be essential. We recommend long sleeves and long trousers throughout the year. This helps protect against scratches, bites or stings. Suitable supportive footwear is essential, no flip-flops, sandals or similar. As a general rule of thumb, layers are best as it is easier to take a layer or two off if you get too warm but difficult to get warm once you have gotten cold. When children have many layers on top but just a pair of trousers, thin socks and wellingtons on the bottom, cold feet and legs are miserable and lead to unhappy participants.

What Forest School is not...

In countries like Denmark they don't 'do' Forest School but 'live' Forest School. It is difficult to import a different culture and many of us running Forest School programmes have embraced the Bridgwater developed concept by using a wide variety of natural environments and developing long-term programmes with primarily child-led learning. These three areas are possibly the key to Forest School, along with well-trained practitioners. The deep learning and growth in self-confidence in all ages at Forest School is amazing. However, learning outside the classroom is happening in many inspirational ways. This can only be positive for children and young people and we need to celebrate all good practice that is taking place out of doors. Therefore, Forest School is not:

- A one-off session or a once a month/term outing.

- Mainly adult-led, planned activities.

- Inflexible planning.

- Lots of non-natural materials or equipment.

- Ill-prepared adults and children.

However, both Forest School and good outdoor learning are rooted firmly in pedagogical theories.

Pedagogical links

Although 'Forest School', as it is widely understood today, is purportedly a recent import in the UK, the philosophy is rooted in many educational theories and theorists on whom modern pedagogy is based. Many theorists believed in experiential and outdoor learning.

Some of the most influential are:

- Friedrich Froebel, in 1818, developed kindergartens – gardens for children, as the best environment for children's learning and development. Froebel believed in child-centred education and teachers should 'begin with where the learner is'. He suggested children should be encouraged to be curious and playful learners rather than being told what to do.

- John Dewey, an American philosopher, believed that children 'learn by doing' and that education should be based on real-life situations. Many of today's curricula that have been developed from Dewey's theory include the UK, Denmark and South Africa.

- Margaret McMillan, along with her sister Rachel, developed an open air nursery in Deptford, London in 1903. This nursery was aimed at improving the health of children from poor families. McMillan provided a mixture of care and

education and believed that space to move and run for a young child was as important as regular meals and sleep. Margaret joined the Froebel society and put great emphasis on the importance of the garden. The children in her care soon improved in both physical and mental well-being.

- Rudolf Steiner again put great emphasis on using the natural environment for creativity and practical experiences such as gardening, baking bread, story and music. Steiner worked with rhythm and routine of days, weeks, years and the seasons.

- Susan Isaac's philosophy was again based on that of Froebel and Dewey. She observed everything the children in her care did and noted that children's play was often linked to real-life experiences as well as natural curiosity. She used the observations to plan for children's learning and followed the children's interests.

- Chris Athey, who was long associated with the Froebel Institute and Pen Green Centre, through practical observation, analysed young children's learning and patterns of behaviour or schema. Identifying schema in young children has become an observational tool in many early years settings and Forest School. Children can be

provided with materials that can support their schemas and once this information is shared with parents or carers, behaviour that may have been found challenging can be recognised and understood. Because of the nature of Forest School, a child's schema is often more easily identified than in other contexts or environments.

These are just a few of the theorists who have shaped modern pedagogical practice today and they all put a strong emphasis on using the outdoors.

In 2006, the UK government published their 'Learning Outside the Classroom Manifesto'. The manifesto states:

'Learning outside the classroom is about raising achievement through an organised, powerful approach to learning in which direct experience is of prime importance. It is not only about what we learn but importantly how and where we learn' (DfES, 2006).

Like much of our curricula and good practice, Forest School builds upon these and many other theories. The emphasis on using the natural environment and practical experiences is a common thread running through the development of early years education and today, the Early Years Foundation Stage (EYFS) gives considerable emphasis and importance to the benefits of well panned outdoor areas.

However from the 1960's, onward there has been a gradual decline in outdoor play spaces and perceived perception of the dangers of letting children play outside. Pound (2009) cites: cars, a fear of abduction, smaller gardens, televisions and electronic toys, alongside a growing intolerance of children's play, as some of the reasons children are less likely to spend time outside. There is a growing body of research that shows many benefits to using the outdoors and in particular the natural environment and yet alongside this research there is more that also shows concern with the decreasing amount of time spent by children in the outdoors. Much has been written about the link between regular use of the outdoors and increased levels of physical activity, higher levels of well-being and a reduction in stress by users of the natural environment.

Whilst working alongside some young parents who used the services of a children's centre, a small-scale research project was undertaken to investigate if these parents allowed their children to play outside. The main reasons given came as a total surprise. All parents had enjoyed playing outside as children and yet none (albeit this was a small sample of ten parents) allowed their own children to play out – except for occasionally in the garden when the weather was fine. Their explanation was that they had been told by 'professionals' they must keep their children clean and provide educational toys. When playing in the garden, making mud pies with a wooden spoon an old bowl was discussed, this did not fit their ideas of 'educational'. One father said he would be afraid his child would be taken into care if the social worker visited and his son was in the garden playing in the mud. An extreme, but never the less very real fear to that parent. He equated this sort of play to neglect: a lesson to be learnt on how important it is for 'professionals' in contact with the vulnerable families, to share how, what and why information is given.

Sheila Sage, one of the main champions of Forest School in Worcestershire writes:

'Most adults, when challenged about a favourite experience from childhood, will recall outdoor experiences as being those most memorable and enjoyable. It has always been a deep personally held belief that children's learning in the outdoors is arguably most effective, because they recognise purpose and enjoy involvement in a more natural environment' (Sage, S. 2011).

We wholeheartedly concur with this sentiment and hope this book inspires you to begin the journey towards seeing for yourself the benefits that Forest School can provide.

MAGICAL MOMENTS

A five-year-old boy, diagnosed with ADHD, but showing no signs at Forest School, on finding a shield bug: "Look everyone I've found a walking leaf".

A four-year-old girl examining the bluebells beginning to bud: "It looks just like an asparagus spear". It does – but we had never made the connection.

A five-year-old boy looking out across a sea of bluebells in the woodland decides to count them: "There's more than ten, there's more than a hundred, there's more than a hundred hundred. There's more than infinity".

A beautiful warm May afternoon and 14 three- and four-year-olds are all busy when one child says: "Sussh, look 'aminals'". The children go quiet and still. About 20 metres outside the perimeter fence two fox cubs had come out to play in the sunshine and were completely oblivious of the children. The children were mesmerised and wanted to find out all about foxes.

Chapter 2: Training and choosing a location

Once you have decided to go down the Forest School route there are two main decisions to be made. Firstly; training – which route is the right for you and your setting – and secondly; the site – where do you plan to run your Forest School sessions? This chapter investigates some of the options.

Training

Having a well-trained workforce is paramount in all industries, but especially so in childcare and education. This is true of those wishing to run a Forest School. There are essentially two main awarding bodies that validate Forest School awards; the Open College Network and EdExcel – although some trainers do work through other awarding bodies. Which route you take depends on where and who you train with.

Once Bridgwater College began running Forest School on a regular basis, the need for specialised training for practitioners was identified and a Level 3 course was developed and validated by Business and Technology Education Council (BTEC) now EdExcel. The staff from the college crèche worked alongside college lecturers to determine the special skills and qualities needed to work in a more challenging and risky environment. These included how to teach the safe use of tools to young children, construction techniques using natural materials, simple shelters, fires and firelighting methods alongside underpinning early years

practitioners, firstly in Worcestershire and shortly afterwards in Oxfordshire. The outreach work has continued to grow and the college now offers training throughout the UK.

As the demand for Forest School training grew, the Forestry Commission Wales invited Forest School leaders, Forestry Commission education officers and Forest School trainers to develop a course that was more adaptable to those working with all ages and a course that had an environmental aspect to it. This new course was validated by the Open College Network (OCN) Wales and is now available through other OCN regions. It is now the most widely available Forest School qualification.

So what does the training involve? Both the BTEC and OCN awards offer three levels of training. The level of training undertaken will depend upon previous experience and qualifications and what you want to do with the qualification on completion.

Open College Network (OCN) Forest School Qualification

Level 3

This award is for practitioners with experience of working with their client group and who wish to lead Forest School sessions either on or off their own site. It takes nine months to complete the award and is roughly equivalent to 'A' level standard.

The award has three units each, worth six credits and sixty learning hours. The hours are a mixture of taught or direct tutor contact and self-directed time.

The three units comprise of:

- Practical skills and woodland management.

- Learning and development at Forest School.

- Delivery and assessment.

The most popular way of offering the course is:

- Five initial days offered consecutively over one week, or one day per week over five weeks.

- Two practical skills days, approximately six weeks later.

and education theories and philosophy. The entry criteria to undertake the course was to have a childcare qualification at Level 3 or above and to be over 21 years of age.

As Forest School continued to develop at Bridgwater College, a Level 2 Assistant award was introduced for those students under 21 years of age or those preferring to act in a supporting role and finally an introductory course at Level 1. This course was aimed initially at parents and carers wishing to learn more about and how to support Forest School sessions. Modules were then devised and incorporated into all the colleges early year's courses.

Originally the BTEC course was designed for early years practitioners, but before long it was realised the Forest School approach would be of benefit to teenage students with special educational needs and especially those with social and emotional difficulties who attended the college. The Forest School staff was soon working with a wide range of clients of all ages especially those who struggled with mainstream education – such as the traveller community, school refusers and those young people attending referral units.

Interest in Forest School continued to grow and in 2000 Bridgwater College delivered training courses for

- A portfolio building workshop and individual tutorial.

- An on-site assessment of the learner leading a Forest School session, approximately six weeks into their programme, is undertaken to ascertain all health and safety requirements are in place, the children's needs are being nurtured and learning is play-based and child-led, as far as possible.

The theoretical aspect of the qualification is produced by compiling a portfolio, but as with all OCN qualifications the evidence can be submitted in a variety of ways and not just written essays. This, together with a copy of the health and safety handbook, is then submitted for marking, moderation and recommendation of accreditation.

Why train?
Reflections from practitioners

Practitioner one, at the end of her initial training days, brought in a lever arch file. In the folder was a collection of research articles and different theories and approaches to practice she had collected over twenty years of teaching.

She said: "*Forest School training has shown me how to put all the theories I have read about and believe in, and amalgamate them into a truly child-centred classroom*".

Practitioner two said: "*I was totally amazed today after learning about how the brain develops and in turn affects our behaviour. The reactions of some children to situations now makes perfect sense and I now have a much calmer reaction to their outbursts*".

Practitioner three said: "*Forest School training has re-ignited my interest and passion for research and theory*".

Practitioner four said: "*Brain development and emotional intelligence have good links to the SEAL (Social and emotional aspects of learning) programme and healthy schools work. I am already finding the relationship I have with the children at Forest School is influencing my classroom teaching in a positive way. There are more moments of connection, more fun and I feel re-enthused about teaching*".

On page 12 is a summary of the personal development and learning during Forest School training by one practitioner.

Forest School training network

As the number of training organisations grew, the Forestry Commission Wales wanted to ensure some quality control over the units they had procured. A training network was developed and organisations wishing to use the Welsh units had to apply to the network and meet certain criteria.

Originally this network was open only to trainers in Wales who met to share good practice and standardisation of marking of portfolios. Some training providers in England felt this network to be valuable practice and therefore membership was extended across the border.

Eventually the network became too large and so England and Wales separated (although the two networks still work very closely together). Prospective trainers apply to the network where a sub-group agree as to whether or not they meet the criteria, and if not, suggest a way forward. The networks review the qualifications on a regular basis and work with OCN to ensure members of the training network deliver training on a reasonable par with each other and therefore offer their learners the best possible experience. The training network also offers a mentoring system to those wishing to become trainers.

Here is a summary by one practitioner of the personal development and learning that took place during Forest School training:

Forest School training reflections

I have realised more about helping children to take risks, that it is 'OK' for them to make mistakes and that they can self risk-assess. I now want to encourage them to take risks in other areas of the curriculum, not just physical risks, but risks in their learning too.

Understanding the benefits of allowing children to initiate their own learning through play. I will use this in my classroom practice.

It has been helpful learning to identify flora and fauna.

I now have a better understanding of what Forest School means and how it can improve children's self-esteem and emotional intelligence. I now want to pass this message onto others.

I have enjoyed learning to tie knots and how to use them. I would now like to pass on these skills to the children in meaningful situations.

Learning about the effects which cortisol, produced by stress, has on the development of children's brains. This was eye opening and has already had an influence on advice which I give to staff in my role as special needs coordinator.

I now realise how important it is to step back and observe the children more. It is hard to let the children take the lead more and not step in too soon.

First aid qualification

An important aspect of becoming a Forest School leader is to ensure you have a suitable first aid qualification – whether you run Forest School on or off your own site. Over the last couple of years there has been some confusion with regard to which first aid course is required. Some of this confusion comes about due to the EYFS statutory requirements and the need for some Forest School practitioners to have a paediatric first aid qualification for in the work place. It is recommended you undertake one of the specialist courses for working in the outdoors. In order to make sure that there is some standardisation within the UK with what is being offered, ITC (Intermediate Temporary Care) has introduced a Forest School first aid course. This course has been accredited by the Health and Safety executive and is offered by various specialist trainers. It is very different coping with the smallest of accidents when you are dealing with the elements or away from running water.

Whichever course you undertake, it needs to have both a paediatric and adult element within it, so having either the first aid at work or a paediatric certificate is not sufficient by itself. Remember you will have both children and other adults at Forest School for whom you will be responsible.

An ideal site

Just as in the Scandinavian countries, Forest School in the UK is taking place in a wide range of environments – both rural and urban. Although ideally this would be a wooded area, this is beyond the reach of many settings. (As previously discussed Forest School in the UK has evolved to be more than the environment: it is an ethos.) Here we will examine an 'ideal' site and a variety of alternative sites that have become successful learning spaces for Forest School.

An ideal site needs to be large enough for the group or groups who are using it and have sufficient diversity to both challenge and sustain the programme, whilst being close enough to walk to from the setting or have safe vehicle access. An area of woodland approximately one to one and half acres, preferably of mixed, mature woodland is a good start. This is about the size of an average football pitch – so not a huge area, but if you are in an urban area it can still prove very difficult. It needs to be large enough to house a base camp seating and fire circle, a semi-permanent shelter for equipment, space for free play and exploration and sufficient variety of trees and shrubs

to provide interest, fuel and materials. Ideally the site will be privately owned and not open to the public. Many sites have a stream or pond within them and this can only enhance the learning opportunities. If possible, some form of secure storage container is useful to save carrying equipment to every session.

FURTHER REFLECTION

Forest School is run successfully in a variety of venues from large estates to pocket parks, in rural and urban sites both publicly and privately owned. Many settings are able to run Forest School in the grounds of their own setting. There are pros and cons to all sites.

Think about your local area. Is there a piece of land locally that could be used? Is there an area of your setting's grounds that is suitable but you haven't really considered it before? Do you have use of a minibus so you can travel slightly further afield? Can parents bring their children straight to an identified area instead of to the setting? Is there a parent/grandparent who may have an area of land that could be utilised? Once a site has been identified, then ownership needs to be established and permission to use the site obtained.

Landowners

Many landowners – from large estates to small independent owners – are very happy for their woodland to be used for Forest School. Oxfordshire Forest School Service, for example, often receives phone calls offering areas which can, in turn, be made available to local groups.

Once an area has been identified, then if possible meet with the landowner or landowner representative in person. Make it clear exactly what experiences you hope the children will have at Forest School. Don't forget the landowner may not have heard of Forest School or may have heard or read the sensational aspects such as young children climbing trees, using tools and lighting fires in the woodland. Discuss boundaries, health and safety, insurance, maintenance and any restrictions of use. Some woodlands may need 'change of use' permissions to enable the area to be used for educational purposes. Once both parties have a verbal understanding then a more formal agreement needs to put in place. The example on page 15 shows the sort of information required by both parties – but is not necessarily exhaustive.

An area within a setting

Many settings have wildlife areas or even wooded areas which are under utilised. Often the wildlife area is fenced off and out of bounds to children – except for the occasional session. If you have an area like this, take a good look at it:

■ Are there trees, shrubs, uneven ground, areas for digging, climbing and exploring?

■ Are there natural paths and an area suitable for a seating circle?

■ Can you import materials to enhance the area?

■ Is there any building work going on at the setting that requires disposal of soil which can be used to make mounds or hillocks?

■ How can the area be developed and who can help?

Watch how the children use different areas of the grounds. If you are in a pre-school setting, try observing the children in the outdoor area without the usual toys, equipment or apparatus:

■ How do they use the space?

■ Do they find areas to hide, to climb, to dig or to play with leaves?

■ Do they use the space differently?

■ Is there an area that naturally lends itself to being used for Forest School?

■ Can spaces be naturally zoned?

If you work within a school environment, again observe the children and how the children use the outdoor spaces:

■ Is the area normally used by your group separated from the main school grounds? If so take the children out to explore the wider environment. Give the children time to investigate their surroundings. Try not to direct activities and let the children take the lead.

■ Do they gravitate to a particular area? Take the children out several times like this on different days and at different times of day. Go out in different weathers and observe if this makes a difference.

Landowner and Governor/Committee Agreement

This agreement is between the Landowner/manager of *insert name of woodland* and the Governing Body/Committee of *insert name of setting*.

Thank you for allowing us to use your woodland. This letter sets the terms and conditions of use of the woodland by the setting and serves as a clear understanding for the parties involved.

Terms and conditions

■ The woodland will be used during term time only. *Insert dates*

■ A maximum of 15 children/young people per session will always be accompanied by a Level 3 qualified Forest School Leader (FSL) with a second practitioner and at least one other adult.

■ A risk assessment will be undertaken by the FSL prior to every session to ensure the wood is safe for the children.

■ The group will not use the wood during windy weather.

■ The health and safety policy will apply at all times. FSLs have a relevant First Aid qualification. They will ensure they have means of communication and an emergency plan should they need to take an injured person out of the wood or evacuate the wood for any reason.

■ Any light management tasks necessary to maintain the safety of the sight will only be undertaken with the agreement and following advice of the landowner or their nominated representative.

■ Occasionally, FSLs will use small fires when conditions permit. FSLs are responsible for ensuring the fire is sited correctly and thoroughly extinguished at the end of the session. If you prefer fires are not lit, please delete.

■ FSLs will organise all sessions so the woodland is left tidy and with minimal environmental impact, with flora and fauna left as undisturbed as possible especially during the nesting/breeding flowering season.

■ All participants are covered by LA/setting insurance *(delete as appropriate)* as part of a 'legitimate activity outdoors', for which parental consent has been obtained.

■ The landowner is required to have public liability insurance for the sum of £5 million. Please include a copy of your insurance certificate with this letter.

Signed on behalf of the landowner _____

Print name _____

Contact telephone no. in case of emergency _____

Signed on behalf of the setting_____

Print name _____

Position held _____

Setting emergency contact and telephone details_____

Thank you. Forest School could not succeed without the generous support of woodland owners/managers. Please sign and return to: *insert details*.

Using a public area

Even in our towns and cities it is surprising how much green and natural usable space there is. It may be a park, a common, a nature reserve or some waste land. Sometimes it is possible to use an area of an allotment, a churchyard or museum garden. Take a good walk around your local area and look the possibilities.

CASE STUDY: BOTLEY SCHOOL, OXFORD

Botley School has a wide catchment area and diverse community – with 27 different first languages being spoken. It has recently merged with the nursery and children's centre – which are on the same site. In one corner of the field was reasonably sized triangle of 'waste' land, probably close to ¾ of an acre, with quite a number of trees. Although this area, not fenced from the playing field, had an unwritten rule that nobody was allowed in without a staff member and hence was not often used. The school decided to use this area for Forest School.

A practitioner in the nursery had trained to be a Forest School leader and had previously taken the children off site. Once a month she also ran Forest School for families from the adjoining children's centre. With help from this group and other parents, the area on the school site was cleared of litter and some of the brambles and a seating circle established. Having a site on the school grounds made Forest School much more assessable and therefore could be offered to more children. All nursery, reception and Key Stage 1 children have a sustained Forest School experience.

To help with the number of sessions, staff members undertook Level 3 leader and assistant leader Level 2 training. The whole staff team, including all support staff, spent an 'outdoor learning' team-building day, including cooking lunch over a campfire, to raise awareness and to gain experience for themselves of the learning opportunities offered in the natural environment. To celebrate the merger with the nursery and official opening, the school held an outdoor learning day when every class spent time at Forest School making vegetable soup or drop scones over the fire. These were shared with parents, carers, siblings and visitors.

The children also planted 200 saplings, one for almost each child in the school, in the adjacent field with help from the local conserver and land manager from the LA environmental centre. This will develop into a substantial area for future use and has been named the 'pen'. A third area, on the opposite side of the field to the original area, has also been left to become more wild. Here they have some fruit trees and allowed the grass to grow long and become colonised with wild flowers. This is called the Apple Grove.

Within six years of embarking down the Forest School route, Botley School now have three very usable areas that all afford different learning experiences for the children. Recently a Swedish-style log cabin has been built as an outdoor classroom and the school is unreservedly embracing the learning opportunities provided by the outdoors.

Botley School, Oxford

Public spaces do have their own issues, but can still provide a rewarding and challenging experience for the children. Many are within a short walking distance of the setting, a definite advantage, saving on both time and transport costs.

The children become very fond and protective of these spaces and therefore a culture of respect for the local environment is fostered at an early age. Families and local groups become involved in looking after the areas which, in turn, has a positive effect on the neighbourhood and community. In Scandinavian countries, local and public areas are regularly the area of choice and use.

Site development and maintenance

Management plan

Whether the site is woodland, an area on your grounds or a public space, an essential aspect of being a Forest School leader is looking after the site you are using. You will be responsible for the health of the environment you use; in the same way as you are responsible for the health of the children and adults in your care. You will be required to

CASE STUDY: A CITY FOREST SCHOOL

We have trained two Forest School leaders and hold continuous Forest School programmes in a local public woodland. We visit the woods every Wednesday morning and each child at the nursery attends for a minimum six-week programme.

We use a local woodland called Ellen's Glen. This is a woodland that has public usage including dog walkers, high school children and shoppers. It is used as a short-cut through to a school and supermarket – it is very urban. The woodland has Local Nature Reserve Status and has a rich habitat including beautiful Wych Elm trees. We work closely with the local woodland ranger employed by The City of Edinburgh Council. We inform her of our visits and email her any new information about the wood. I like the children to know someone cares for the woodland. Jess, the ranger, will occasionally visit a session and we plant trees and wild flowers provided by her.

Pros of using a public site:

- Children get to know a local woodland very well and can visit it as often as they want.

- We can take advantage of a mature woodland with many tree species, wild flowers and birds. We have heard a woodpecker and regularly see dippers. There is also a river.

- We are able to work with The Ranger Service, who are very supportive to us and the local Forest Education Initiative cluster group.

- We act as a model for people passing by who often want to know what we are doing.

- We do a litter sweep in the bit of the wood we use the night before Forest School. This must be a positive thing for this habitat.

Cons of using a public site:

- Dogs can be a problem. We have to make sure that there is no dog excrement and we sometimes have dogs running through the site. We make a point of getting to know all dog walkers.

- A large amount of litter is dropped each week as people pass through the wood. We have to pick this up the evening before we use the site.

- Anti-social behaviour comes and goes at this site. We are having a good period at the moment. However we have had to cope with fires, trees being slashed, the dumping of prams and shopping trolleys etc.

- The litter and vandalism can be time consuming for us as we have to check and clear the site in preparation for every visit.

However, for us, the pros greatly outweigh the cons and we are all very fond of this special area of urban woodland.

Written by Ros Marshall, Nursery Teacher, Liberton Nursery School in Edinburgh

produce a site management plan as part of your leadership assessment, as well as an ecological impact survey. The management plan is usually written for three years and will include the proposed development of the site, action and review. This does not have to be overly complicated. (See examples on page 20.)

Tree safety check

Before anyone can use the site, the trees in the area should be checked by a competent person. The landowner may prefer to do this or you may need to arrange for a certified tree surgeon or forester to carry this out. If you are using a local authority site, they may have a specialist person who will carry out the check. Either way, this may incur a charge – not only for the inspection but for any work that may be identified.

Once the site is being used, a visual check is made by the leader on a regular basis especially after high winds and a more formal check, usually bi- or three-yearly, built into the site management plan.

Boundaries

There are many ways to define the area within which the children will have free range. It may be the area has a natural hedgerow bordering the entire area, a stream or pathways that are easily identified, but if not, you need to decide on a strategy to establish the boundaries of your site. This can be a permanent or temporary boundary.

Here are some ways practitioners have adopted:

- Permanent fencing: including chestnut paling, stock fencing, hazel hurdles, post and rail, post and rope, chain link or even large boulders.

- Temporary fencing may have to be put up and taken down at each session. It can be rope stretched between trees, marker tape or homemade markers. There is a safety issue to leaving rope up between sessions on a public site in case people are injured by not seeing it and walking into it. It could be something as simple as the grass is not mown in the Forest School area and children don't venture onto the adjacent mown areas during the session. See Case study: Markers, on page 21.

See Case study: Markers, on page 21.

CASE STUDY: DENMARK

A large 120 place day nursery in an urban setting takes 20 of the older children; five-six year olds, to an allotment. The same children go every day, all day, for six months.

The facilities are very basic. There is a wooden hut, built by one of the pedagogues and funded by the local authority, which houses a basic chemical toilet and a wood-burning cooker which provides heat and where simple food can be cooked.

The outdoor area is just as simple. There is a small glasshouse where children grow tomatoes and peppers and various other containers for growing a variety of fruit and vegetables.

As in most Danish settings, there is a large area with sand and earth for digging. Child-sized spades, buckets, rakes and trowels, made of metal and very sturdy, are readily available for use. Here children have the space to use their gross motor skills and can use their imagination to construct quite intricate and imaginary worlds. The beauty of these large digging areas is there is space for large constructions where children can work alone or in groups and the creations can be left and built upon over a sustained period of time. Small metal wheelbarrows are also available and I observed the children using these to help the pedagogues create a gravel path around the hut.

There is the essential outdoor fire pit and seating circle, a wood store, a rope swing hanging from the branch of a tree and lots of stone, rocks and boulders. The children are all happy, calm and engrossed in various self-instigated pursuits.

CASE STUDY: FINLAND

The nursery is situated on the edge of an office and light industrial estate. The indoor space is a converted office containing a sleep room, kitchen and dining space, a small baby room, various open-plan spaces with lots of books and natural materials. Outside is a veranda with coat pegs for outdoor clothing and boots. The outdoor space is not attached to the building but across the road and this is where the parents drop the children off in the morning.

There is a picket fence with pegs where children hang their rucksacks. Each child brings a rucksack to nursery including; a flask containing a warm drink, a snack and a folding 'sit upon'. The pedagogues greet the children in the garden and the children are free to play immediately. The area has no grass or tarmac but is simply compacted soil. There are two fire pits with seating circles, a wooden shelter where the babies sleep during the day, a wooden shed containing a first aid kit, skis (for winter) and simple equipment such as ropes and tools.

On this day, at 9am the key workers gather their children around the fire circles and discuss the day. The youngest children remain in the garden area. The older group, five/six-year-olds, stay near the nursery, but outside of the garden, to have a creative day. This is still outside in the public grassed area, which includes a large pond. The three- and four-year-olds head to the equivalent of Forest School. They collect their rucksacks and head off along a public footpath. The children are allowed to run ahead and have various landmark points where they wait for everyone else.

On reaching 'Forest School', the children choose which area they go to. There are three areas, all public spaces. They choose 'the rocky place'. There are quite steep slopes and rocks for them to climb but they all mange remarkably well. The children again are free to roam and explore. There are no physical boundaries but the children know their limits. They come together for snack and hot drink, which is provided by their parents. They all manage their own flask and pour their own drink. This is a social time with lots of conversation between friends. Another class of students, this time teenagers, arrive and sit close by for their snack. Neither group takes any notice of the other. The teenagers are quiet and respectful.

After a few minutes they move off and nursery children put away their flasks and continue with their play. The pedagogue has a rucksack with basic equipment that the children can ask for if they wish to use it. After a while, two girls ask for paper and pencils to draw some flowers they have found. Another two ask for knives to do some whittling. They know exactly how to sit and use the knives.

The children come together again later with flasks and bowls and sit on their mats. This time they take 'dinner gloves' out of their rucksacks. (The weather is often too cold for the children to remove gloves for hand washing or eating and therefore by having clean gloves they remain warm, comfortable and reasonably hygienic.) The children help themselves to a bowl and serve themselves pasta and vegetable stew from the wide-neck flasks. The cook from the setting has produced the meal and brings it in a handcart to a designated area to be collected by the group. This happens every day.

After lunch, the lead pedagogue takes a small lantern from his rucksack and lights a tee light. He builds up the anticipation of a story by inviting an imaginary fairy to join the children.

After listening to today's story, everyone collects up their belongings, plates and flasks and heads back down to the path and the awaiting cart. Again the children are allowed to run on ahead, waiting at the usual landmarks. On returning to the nursery the children take off their outdoor clothing, go to the bathroom and strip to their thermal underwear. They climb into giant multi-person bunk beds where they have an afternoon rest.

Example of a simple management plan

Year one	Proposed development	Action	Review date
Sept-July	Survey of flora and fauna in the site	Identify flora and fauna as the year progresses. Take photographs where possible.	Yearly
Aug	Undertake tree safety check	Contact tree surgeon.	Every other year
Sept	Undertake ecological impact survey	Write survey for handbook.	Termly
Sept	Create seating circle	Involve children in deciding the best area for the base camp. Contact sources and suppliers for materials.	Termly
Year Two	Plant native hedgerow to divide Forest School from field	Apply to Woodland Trust for native hedgerow pack.	
Year Three	Coppice hazel	Sort into various thicknesses. Make new mallets.	

Example of a Ecological Impact Matrix

Activity	Macro Fauna	Micro Fauna	Soil	Ground layer flora	Field layer flora	Shrub layer flora	Canopy layer flora
Moving around site	Disturbance especially during the breading season	Trampled upon. Loss of habitat.	Erosion/ Compaction	Trampled	Damage	Damage	N/A

Macro Fauna – mammals and birds. Micro Fauna – invertebrates.

Insurance

The landowner will require public liability insurance to a minimum of £5,000,000 and the setting should inform their insurance company that they are running Forest School sessions. Most insurance companies are happy for Forest School to be a normal part of pre-school life. However some insurance companies restrict what experiences the children can have at Forest School or restrict the age at which they can participate with using tools or having a fire. (It seems strange that insurance companies may put restrictions on the use of knives or tools at Forest School under the supervision of specifically-trained staff, but not impose restrictions on a woodwork bench or cooking in the setting.)

Health and hygiene

The welfare of all those attending Forest School is of paramount importance within a framework of understanding and managing risk. The site needs to be checked on a daily usage basis to remove any hazards especially where the site has public access.

As part of the assessment criteria for the Level 3 Leader qualification, a health and safety handbook has to be produced. This will become the leader's essential tool and most-trusted working document. Policies and procedures are available for reference by all concerned and risk assessments collated for the experiences undertaken by the children.

CASE STUDY: MARKERS

One setting uses markers made by the children. Their Forest School area is within a large woodland bordered on one side by a lake. The Forest School leader discussed with the children the best way they could be reminded not to wander too far away or too near the lake. The children thought flags would be a good idea, so once back at school they drew patterns onto A4 sheets of paper and stapled them onto hazel stakes. Each week they carry them to Forest School and placed the flags at strategic points around the negotiated boundary. At the end of the session the flags are collected up and taken back to school. Eventually the paper flags were replaced by cloth, again made by the children. A simple and effective idea; but giving children ownership and responsibility for their own and others safety.

Our 'risk adverse' society has resulted in the term 'cotton wool kids' but children need to develop self-awareness and self-regulation by learning the meaning of risk and managing hazards. Risk assessments can be written in many ways and it is best to follow the format already used by your setting or local authority. It is natural to try to protect our children but by involving them in understanding and therefore managing risk from the beginning, safety becomes second nature to them. They are quick to see how best to do things and manage different situations – resulting in some 'deep-level' thinking and problem solving. It is good practice to add the risk benefit to the assessment. When assessing risk you need to decide which ones are acceptable and which are not for your client group. For example, if it has been raining is it still ok to climb the trees? If so, why, and if not, why not? However, what other opportunities does the rain afford? It is surprising how quickly children accept responsibility and are quick to remind not only each other but visiting adults of the 'rules'.

One essential piece of equipment required by the leader is a health and safety rucksack. Depending on whether the Forest Site is on, close to or remote from the setting, will determine the equipment needed. Typically this will contain a first aid kit, spare clothing/welfare kit, folding trowel, emergency blanket, storm shelter, torch (preferably wind-up), small can of cola drink and emergency details. These rucksacks can be purchased complete from Forest School equipment suppliers or made up to one's own requirements.

Health and safety game

Adults often worry children may get lost at Forest School. Bridgwater College developed a game called 'One, two, three, where are you?' which has been used by many children since. From the very beginning of the programme the children are taught the game. At first it may be an adult who hides. The Forest School leader will then ask the children: "Does anyone know where Jenny is?". When they answer "no" he/she will say: "Let's call loudly one, two, three, where are you?". The children all call loudly and hear Jenny reply "one, two, three I'm over here". The children all run to find Jenny. Everyone returns to base camp and the leader explains to the children that if they ever feel unhappy or feel lost to stay very still and call in a loud voice "one, two, three, where are you?". It is then time for the children to have a turn at hiding. The children love this game and never tire of playing it but also understand it has serious application. At first the children often cannot locate where the answer is coming from but over the weeks they become much more accurate in detecting the direction of the sound, useful in developing their listening skills.

CASE STUDY: HEALTH AND SAFETY GAME

Emily, a four-year-old, had been attending Forest School about four months. Her mum knew about the 'One, two, three' game from what the leader had told parents during the information session held for parents before the children attended Forest School. She had also taken a turn on the parent rota so had seen it in practice.

One day whilst shopping in the supermarket with Emily they became separated. Just as mum realised Emily was no longer with her – she heard a voice calling "one, two, three, where are you mum?". Emily's mum was quickly able to follow the voice to find her daughter. She was really impressed Emily had remained calm and had transferred skills learnt at Forest School into everyday life.

Toileting and hand washing

This is probably one of the things that worry adults almost more than any other subject at Forest School. We have found that if children visit the toilet before leaving the setting it not very often they will need to go before the end of the session. However there are times when children will need to visit the toilet and there are many solutions to how this is managed. Whichever way is chosen it should be managed as sensitively as possible. To some extent the solution is dependent on the site being used. If you are using an area of your grounds then it will be possible to return to the setting. This needs to be managed and risk assessed if it takes a member of staff away from group. How does it affect ratios of those left at Forest School?

Private woodlands can possibly have a composting toilet or pit latrine. These need to be at least 50 metres from any water course. A designated 'peeing' area can be created behind screen, either temporary or semi-permanent and in an area not used for other purposes. Dig a trench and fill with straw. Charcoal can be placed on top as this helps to neutralise the urine. If a child needs to defecate take them to a quiet area, preferably just outside the site. Dig a hole at least a trowels depth, in which the child can go. After use, refill in the hole with soil and cover the area to leave as natural as possible.

If you are using a public site and you are unable to bury the faeces it will need to be taken away. The easiest way is to put a plastic bag over a potty. When the child has finished, securely seal the plastic bag and place inside a second bag (double bagging). Dispose of responsibly. Make sure hands are washed after going to the toilet, before eating or preparing food. Soap and water is the best method. If you have a shelter or storage on your site it is easy to have a small washing up bowl and bring a flask of warm water and towel with you. During the summer you can have a container of water on site. If you have to bring everything with you a small collapsible camping bowl is very handy and light to carry as are lightweight camping hand towels. Use an eco-friendly soap which is kinder to the environment when you tip the water away. Hang the towel in the fresh air which inhibits bacterial growth. Wipes are not very effective and create a lot of waste and anti-bacterial gel should only be used on clean hands – they will not wash off mud and dirt.

Waterproof clothing

An essential aspect of health and safety is too ensure everyone at Forest School is suitably dressed against the weather. Some children and adults in the UK do not necessarily have suitable outdoor clothing, unlike those in many of the Scandinavian countries. Many children go from

warm homes, into a warm car and straight into a warm setting and therefore do not need wet or cold-weather clothing which is often expensive. Settings approach the need in many ways:

- Ask parents to provide suitable clothing as part of the uniform

- Secure sponsorship from local businesses to buy waterproofs

- Raise funds to provide waterproofs

- Local authority waterproof lending schemes.

I recommend that it is more important to provide waterproof trousers or dungarees than jackets. Most children have a reasonable jacket to wear but if we expect children to sit on logs and play happily in mud then the bottom half of the child needs to be warm and dry. Equally, adults also need to be warm and dry and many settings acknowledge this by providing adequate clothing for staff and volunteers. This also shows the adults are valued for the role they play at Forest School. As mentioned before, there is a well-known saying 'there is no such thing as bad weather, only bad clothing'. After observing many Forest School sessions, we believe this to be true.

TOP TIP

Don't forget the adults. Practitioners and volunteers need to be a appropriately dressed as well. Have a set of generic waterproofs that any adult going outside can quickly put on.

The fire circle

The heart of Forest School is the base camp or fire circle. Not every site can have a permanent fire circle but the holistic development that takes place around the fire is phenomenal. There is nothing quite like the experience of sitting around the campfire enjoying a drink and snack, listening to the sounds of the crackling fire, the smell of the smoke and the glow of the coals. It is a place to share feelings, tell and listen to stories or have a sing-song. Quotes from children sitting by the campfire:

"The trees look all wobbly through the smoke."

"The fire sounds cross" (listening to the fire crackling).

Looking at the ashes: *"The fire has died to a zebra"*.

There are many examples of fire circles, but this example seems to work well with young children. Fires do not have to very big for most sessions. A square of logs or circle of fire bricks or igneous rocks to form an area approximately 60-75 centimetres in diametre is sufficient. House bricks or concrete blocks are not suitable as these can explode when heated. A second row of logs, a child's arm length outside the inner logs is a good idea for young children. They can kneel on these logs and cook safely using a whittled stick. Seating logs can be placed an adult stride away from the outer row. Make sure clear exits are left in case of emergency.

There are different ways that seating logs can be made. The simplest way is log slices approximately 25-30 centimetres and 30 centimetres high. If you can source a tree trunk, this can be laid where you want the seating and pegged at either end. To make the pegs simply pare one end of each of four sticks, like paring a pencil. Bang the pared end into the ground close to the log, one either side at each end. Lash the two pegs together using a figure of eight motion. The lashing and stakes stops the log from rolling when being sat upon. Cradles can be made to house planks or logs can be partially buried in the ground, a notch cut out of a half log which fits over the log and then fixed with nails. (See illustration on page 24 for an example.)

Know the rules

Make sure you have permission from the landowner to have a fire. Site the area away from hazards like overhanging branches and clear the area from leaf litter and debris. Keep in mind the weather conditions and do not light a fire during very dry or windy conditions. Remember conditions can change during the session and the fire should never be left unattended.

Ensure children know and understand the rules. Never walk within the seating circle. Practise approaching the circle from the outside and step over the seating log and then sit down. Reverse this to exit the area. Make sure adults follow the rules as well and always demonstrate safe practice. During early days at Forest School, how to approach the fire circle can be practiced through playing games to change places

Camp fire showing a variety of seating options

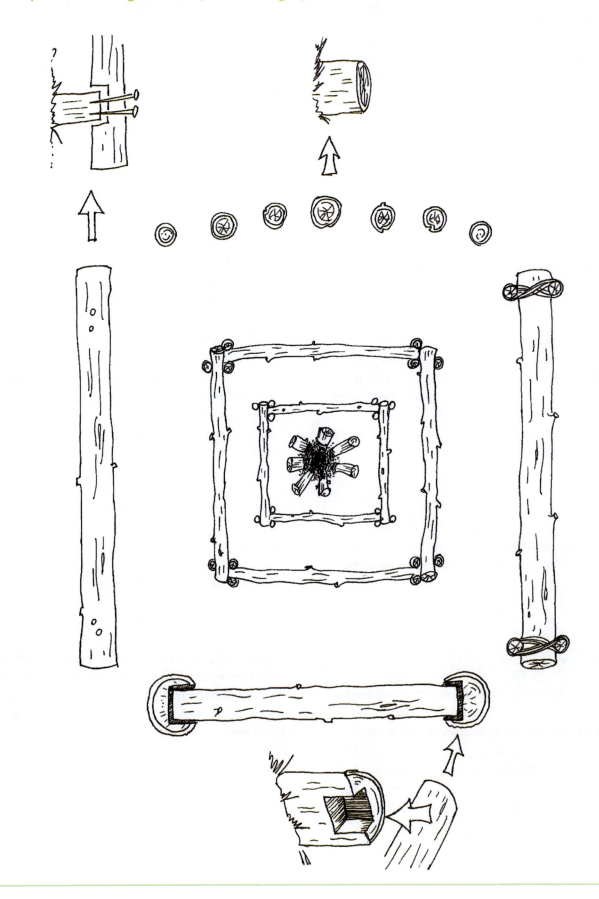

around the circle. Remember, however, that the idea of 'a fire' may be a very abstract conception to some children so light a small fire fairly soon into the programme, to enable children to have a true understanding and meaning of the fire circle. You will also be able to judge the reactions of the group and whether the fire causes too much anxiety for anyone. One day, four-year-old became very distressed when the fire was lit. None of the staff at the setting realised there had been a fire in her home approximately six months earlier. Over the following months her fear gradually lessened and with the support of sensitive staff she eventually felt confident enough to cook over the fire.

If possible, have a log store so there is a always a good supply of dry, seasoned wood.

Get the children to help collect fuel. Explain and show them the difference between 'green' or fresh wood and dead wood.

Firstly collect **tinder**; small twigs, wood shavings, dry leaves, bullrush heads, silver birch bark or similar that will ignite easily and help to keep the fire going. Next you will need **kindling**. Ask the children to gather sticks no thicker than their finger, no longer than their hand. Adults can gather dry standing, dead wood from trees. This is placed over the tinder in a pyramid or teepee shape. Then the main **fuel** is needed, larger pieces of wood that will burn for longer periods of time. The children can collect wood no thicker than their wrist, no longer than their forearm or if they are ready to use tools, then a bow-saw can be introduced to cut up longer branches. As you can see this quickly turns into a mathematical exercise; as the children are measuring and estimating against parts of their bodies. Once the kindling and wood is collected, it can be sorted by size. Different types of wood have different wood-burning properties and it is useful to know these properties. For example; elder, sweet chestnut, cedar, hemlock, balsam, spruce and the pines all spit hot cinders into the air. This can be dangerous for the children seated nearby.

On this page is the poem *Woods for burning* to help children (and adults) remember the differences.

Putting it out

Before you light a fire, make sure you have the means of putting it out. It is recommended that a minimum of ten

Woods for burning

Logs to burn! Logs to burn!
Logs to save the coal a turn!
Here's a word to make you wise
When you hear the woodsman's cries.

Beech wood fires burn bright and clear,
Hornbeam blazes too,
If the logs are kept a year
To season through and through.

Oak logs will warm you well
If they are old and dry.
Larch logs of the pine smell
But the sparks will fly.

Pine is good and so is Yew
For warmth through winter days,
But poplar and the willow too
Take long to dry or blaze.

Birch logs will burn to fast,
Alder scarce at all,
Chestnut logs are good to last
If cut in the fall.

Holly logs will burn like wax –
You should burn them green.
Elm logs like a smoldering flax,
No flames to be seen.

Pear logs and apple logs
They will scent a room,
Cherry logs across the dogs
Smell like flowers in bloom.

But ash logs all smooth and grey,
Burn them green or old,
Buy up all that come your way
They're worth their weight in gold!

Unknown

Involve parents in cooking sessions. A variety of foods from different cultures can easily be cooked over the campfire and encourages children to try new tastes.

five-year-olds were able to experience making and lighting their own fire. Then there is a whole variety of fire bowls, some made from clay but the majority from steel.

Cooking over the fire is a very satisfying experience for both adults and children and it is very easy to cook simple, wholesome food linking to the healthy schools agenda. There is growing concern over the number of obese children so encouraging good habits whilst young and in a fun way will hopefully lay down good habits for the future. Simple breads, quesadillas, quick soups and drop scones are all easy to cook and popcorn is always exciting. There are many campfire cookbooks available on the market but everyday recipes can be adapted. Food can also be foraged and incorporated into cooking. Fruit and berries are easily sourced and cooked in drop scones or pancakes. Elderflowers are turned into fritters, wild garlic added to soups, nettles made into tea or wilted like spinach, sweet chestnuts roasted and of course the many types of edible fungi. It goes without saying you need to be absolutely certain you know what you are picking and preferably away from roadsides and exhaust fumes.

litres of water is available. Pond, stream or rainwater is ideal. As an extra precaution, have a fire blanket in your health and safety rucksack. If you have a permanent site you could also have a fire beater.

Once the fire has died down, carefully spread the embers, using a stick, within the fire pit area. Sprinkle the area liberally with water. Once the steam has died down, hold the palm of your hand just above the embers. If any heat can still be felt, douse again. Stir up the embers to uncover any hot spots and check again. Make sure all the debris is cold before the area is left.

Leave no trace of fire

If you are not using an established fire pit area, make sure you leave the area as natural looking as possible. Once the fire is fully extinguished, collect up the ashes and scatter as wide as possible. Cover the spot with soil and leaf litter to conceal the fact a fire had been lit.

If you are unable to have a permanent fire area there are many ways you can still give children the experience of having a fire. For example, tiny fires made on scallop shells. The fire does not last very long but the children, four- and

Shelters

Shelters, although not essential, are a useful enhancement to a Forest School site and again there are many types of shelter used. Many private sites are able to have a semi-permanent shelter. Although semi-permanent, if they are well made they can last for many years and provide: shelter during inclement weather, a base for coats, simple equipment, washing facilities or wood storage. Others put up a tarpaulin or storm shelter as and when necessary. These are usually quickly erected either between trees or using poles and guy ropes then taken down again at the end of the session. Occasionally Scandinavian-style log cabins are built. These are much more permanent and substantial, but can only be built on private sites or school grounds. In some cases shelters are built of purely natural materials. These can be very simple lean-to shelters to more complex round houses and everything in between.

After you have undertaken this training and developed your site, you can enjoy your Forest School sessions. Joseph Cornell, one of the most highly regarded nature educators in the world today says that "keeping children inside one room five days a week is akin to breaking a horse". Relax and delight in the learning you will see unfold before you.

CASE STUDY: SHELTERS

A group of Key Stage 2 students from a pupil referral unit had been attending Forest School on a weekly basis, for six months.

Den-building was one of their favourite activities.

They had experimented with many different designs. At school they had been studying the Celts and their round houses and asked if they could build a round house at Forest School. They planned the design and sourced the materials from the wider woodland with the help of the woodland manager.

Over six weeks they worked together – in itself a major achievement, and built the round house with willow walls and a bender style roof.

They were very proud of the finished product and were pleased to find, when they returned the following week; it had been used by the younger children.

At the end of the year, it was arranged for them to visit Forest School to see the younger children using their creation. It gave a real boost to the self-esteem of these young people, all of whom had been excluded from mainstream education, to see their hard work appreciated.

The pre-school and nursery children were equally as pleased to find the 'big' children had built a house for them.

It was used for all sorts of imaginary and role play, as well as becoming a favourite place for stories. One week it was a supermarket where the ingredients to make bread were sold. Another week it was the cave where 'bear' lived and the children reenacted *We're going on a bear hunt*.

Top: from this case study; middle: shelter with public access; bottom: shelter on a multi-use site

Chapter 3: First steps to Forest School

Organising Forest School sessions

Developing a Forest School programme is an evolutionary process, often becoming more established as the practitioners and children develop their skills and knowledge. When developing a Forest School, it is important to look not only at where the child is at, but also assess the skills and knowledge of families and the setting itself.

Forest School provision will differ from setting to setting, and will be as unique as the staff, children and family who form it. There is, however, a general ethos that Forest School practitioners should follow (see Chapter 1). What works in one setting may not work in another. The most important thing is that children and adults are enjoying and benefiting from their time in the natural world.

How often sessions take place and for how long, will depend on a number of factors. Finding a Forest School site that offers suitable challenge and is accessible for children with mobility issues, may be problematic. Class sizes and staffing costs associated with maintaining the 1:4 ratio, as well as training and transport, also need consideration. Bentsen et al. (2010) note that these 'economic' and 'cultural barriers' also affect udeskole in Denmark (Bentsen et al. 2010, p.6).

Recently, educational settings in the UK have been supported by government in taking learning outdoors and off-site. DEFRA (2011) notes that the government's White Paper, 'The Importance of Teaching', will:

> '…free teachers from unnecessary statutory duties creating more opportunities for different routes to learning, including learning outside the classroom' (DEFRA, 2011, p.47).

According to the report by DEFRA (2011), schools should feel entitled to teach outdoors whenever 'they wish to do so' and that in collaboration with the Health and Safety Executive, the government aims 'to remove unnecessary rules and other barriers to learning in the natural environments'.

Best practice in organising a Forest School session

The following elements should all be present in order to run a Forest School session:

- Trained Forest School leader (trained to Level 3 or higher)

- Regular use of a natural site for a sustained period of time

- Small groups, high ratio of adults to children (1:4 is the recommended ratio)

- Established base camp – a central meeting point where resources are kept

- Freedom for child-led exploration and play

- Carefully planned learning, tailored to the children's interests and needs

- Group games to build social skills, relationship and trust

- A flexible plan with routine and familiarity

- Plans should include practitioners', parents' and children's ideas and perspectives.

Example structure

- Initial sessions will have a focus on establishing boundaries and safety

- Children will be encouraged to play and explore the environment using all of their senses

- Social games are often introduced to build relationships, trust and collaborative play between the participants

- A small achievable task is set by the Forest School leader during the session to help scaffold or broaden the childrens' experiences, build knowledge or to develop a new skill.

Initial Forest School sessions

Beckie Shuttleworth is a teacher and Forest School trained leader in Fulham. Her introductory plan for a block of six sessions are appropriate for Foundation Stage or Key Stage classes. The focus is to help the children settle safely and securely into their Forest School environment.

Beckie's Foundation and Key Stage 1 Introductory Plan can be found on page 89 in the appendices.

You will notice that each session is not overly detailed but there is enough information to remind her of her focus for the session. The majority of the session will be spent engaging in spontaneous learning that arises from following the children's interests and lines of inquiry.

Friends Forest Nursery in Surrey also offers introductory sessions to support children in learning the boundaries and how to keep themselves safe, particularly around the fire.

Much of this knowledge and these skills are gained through games and marking boundaries on trees with bows. Tool safety is practiced daily with children having opportunities to peel carrots and apples.

However, unlike Beckie's School, Forest School leaders at Forest Friends Nursery do not record Forest School plans on paper. They plan verbally through conversations with colleagues and children.

Graffham Infants and Duncton CE Juniors Forest School's sessions are planned by incorporating a mixture of children's interests, curiosity and questioning as well as progression of skills throughout the age range; leading on from teacher-planned learning and leading on from the previous weeks' session.

Forest School provision in different early years settings

Williams-Siegfredson (2005 cited in Maynard, 2007) describes that although most nurseries in Denmark incorporate the instruction of nature and natural phenomena, there are vast differences as to how this is accomplished.

Maynard (2007) notes that there are Danish Forest nurseries or nature kindergartens which are located in woodland, additionally, there are nurseries that have 'wood groups' which visit woodland sites on a weekly basis and those that use their own outdoor space for Forest School provision (p.320).

Similarly, there are various models of outdoor kindergartens in Sweden, Norway, Germany and the UK, some of which offer total immersion, while others offer weekly visits. Although there is a difference in how Forest School is delivered in settings, the theoretical underpinning should be the same throughout.

Forest School programmes have been implemented with children of all ages and abilities in settings across the UK.

Settings in the UK

The following six case studies are examples of how Forest School programmes have been achieved.

CASE STUDY: FOREST SCHOOL SESSIONS IN WEST SUSSEX

We arrive and the older children unload the Land Rover and set up the base camp. This includes creating a shelter, fire and equipment.

The junior children know that they have to stay in sight of the fire and must not cross the stream without an adult. However, with the younger children, we discuss and tie boundary bows to mark areas they must keep within.

When the younger children first arrive they help collect fire kindling and wood to get the fire started or support adults in setting up the shelter and equipment. Every session always has a fire.

Occasionally, the nursery and reception class children work up to using a fire, at the beginning of their sessions if we feel they need the progressions.

After base camp is set, we discussion activities and go through new skills to be taught and then there is free play. About 30% of the session is adult supported and 70% is child initiated from a range of supported activities.

We have hot chocolate and biscuits about an hour into the session to replenish our energy levels and warm our bodies on a cold day.

We continue with our activities and play and then come together in a circle to discuss the session and reflect on our experiences and learning.

We end the session by collaboratively packing up the equipment and leaving our camp in the natural state we found it.

We then head back to school. Back at school, children are encouraged to share their experiences with the adults, peers and parents. Some of the experiences from Forest School may be used to develop classroom-based work or learning.

The school regularly celebrates pupils' achievements both inside and outside the classroom.

Helen Martin, a headteacher from West Sussex

CASE STUDY: FOREST SCHOOL IN PRIVATE LOCAL WOODLAND

This Forest School site is a private woodland located one mile away from the schools. It takes approximately five minutes to get to the site by minibus.

The same group of children go out for six sessions, in a six-week block (mornings or afternoons). Every child in the school from three years to 11 years participates in a block of sessions per year. The children are out for two-three hours at a time.

The sessions are run throughout the year apart from when the forest is being used for pheasant shooting between October and February. Consequently, the forest is used for four weeks in September; and then again from February to July. The Forest School leaders have found that children in Years 3 and 4 are better able to cope with the colder weather between February to March.

They take cohorts out together even if they have a mixed-age class. Cohorts consist of approximately 15 children, which this setting have found to be the most number of children in to have in the forest at one time. Their ratios are as follows:

- Four adults to 15 children, or approximately 1:4 for Year 2 and up.

- Six adults to 15 children, or approximately 1: 2 or 1:3 for nursery, reception class and Year 1.

Both schools approach parents to volunteer, and so improve ratios for the younger children. Parent helpers who have previously worked with the school and share the culture and understanding of forest schooling are invited to participate.

There are three Forest School trained staff comprising of the headteacher, assistant headteacher and nursery manager; although, two more staff will be trained soon. Many education settings train additional colleagues as the provision grow. This will ensure the programme is sustained if colleagues are absent or move on to different roles.

Graffham Infants and Duncton CE Juniors Forest School, West Sussex.

CASE STUDY: FOREST SCHOOL IN A LONDON PARK

Although the centre did not have a trained Forest School leader, the headteacher Kathryn had heard of a Forest School pilot programme run by Forest School qualified park rangers at Holland Park.

A group of six to ten children were identified to participate, based on practitioners identification of the children most in need of such an experience.

The centre's ratio for outings is 1:2 or 1:1 for children with special educational needs (SEN).

- These children travelled with staff, parents and student volunteers to Holland Park on public transport, once a week for six weeks.

- They spent from 9:30am-2:30pm at Holland Park, participating in a range of Forest School activities and eating their picnic lunch outdoors.

Staff and parents at the centre noticed an improvement in children's behaviour.

- Children who showed challenging behaviour in the setting were much more relaxed and focused at Forest School.

- Insecure or quiet children were more communicative and engaged and parents commented how much their children were sharing their learning at home.

Although the pilot has ended, children and staff from Chelsea Open Air Nursery School and Children's Centre continue to attend Forest School sessions at Holland Park.

Money is reserved from the centre's budget for children to attend two hour sessions.

Chelsea Open Air Nursery School and Children's Centre, London.

CASE STUDY: FOREST SCHOOL ON A UNIVERSITY CAMPUS

For many of the families using the centre, living accommodation is cramped and few have access to a garden at home.

Eastwood Nursery first set up its Forest School in February 2006 on Barnes Common. However, limitations with the site proved to be problematic for the group and the Forest School leaders looked for more accessible space for the children.

In September 2006, with permission, Eastwood started using the grounds of Roehampton University grounds. They formed a link with Redford House Nursery (which was part of Roehampton University). The two settings met up for 'Forest School' on a weekly basis. This encouraged new opportunities for children and adults to work collectively, and inspire and learn from each other. Unfortunately, Redford House Nursery closed permanently but Eastwood has continued to develop their Forest School provision.

The centre currently has seven (Level 3) trained leaders, many of whom provide outreach or consultancy support to schools and centres across London in developing urban Forest School programmes. Forest School leaders also run a number of sessions for families living in the community.

Their Forest School site at Roehampton University is not technically woodland; however, the staff report children refer to it as a 'forest' as it is a large space. The site is located at the centre of the community and is ten minute walk from the centre. Over the last four years, the provision has evolved. Today, children from across the centre from 10 months to five years attend Forest School sessions. Groups of children aged three-five years old, go out twice a week for up to two hours. In 2011, the nursery school successfully started offering all day Forest School sessions for the oldest children in the centre during the spring and summer term. Children under three, go out once a week for up to two hours each session. The ratio of adults to children for children under three-years-old is 1:3 and for children three years old and over it is 1:4. They are able to maintain high ratios by having the support of supernumeraries, parents and student volunteers.

Working parents are given opportunities to participate with their children on Saturday Forest School sessions. The centre also hosts 'Parents and Parks Days' throughout the year where parents join their children in a local park for the day, participating in outdoor play and Forest School related activities.

Eastwood Nursery School Centre for Children and Families, Borough of Wandsworth, London.

CASE STUDY: FOREST SCHOOL IN THE CENTRE'S GROUNDS AND IN NATURE RESERVE

Children from two-years-old and up participate hour-long Forest School sessions on-site within the centre's grounds.

Children are offered a block of six sessions as part of their Forest School experience; however, there are opportunities for children to participate in additional sessions. All sessions are led by Forest School leaders. Children aged three- to five-years-old also attend sessions in the centre's grounds; however, on the sixth session, the children spend a day out at Hammersmith and Fulham's largest local Nature Reserve, Wormwood Scrubs. The centre uses a wooded area known as the Kops within Wormwood Scrubs. The children walk to the site and take the bus back to the centre. It takes approximately 40 minutes for the children to reach

the site by foot so the bus ride back gives them an opportunity to recover from all the exercise. The ratio of adults to children is 2:6; although, children with Special Educational Needs are given one to one support.

It was decided by the centre's teams to take children out on the sixth session because they felt it would make the sessions more inclusive and accessible to all children. leaders had noticed that children needed to be familiar with the staff and Forest School activities in the centre before they were able to make the transition of using a space off-site.

Randolph Beresford Children's Centre, Borough of Hammersmith and Fulham, London.

CASE STUDY: FOREST SCHOOL ON PRIVATE LAND

Every pre-school child goes once a week in term time. Babies from three months to three-years-old go out every day to build stamina; again all year round in all weathers. Sessions run from 9.15am to 12.30pm. The nursery uses three sites, 5mins walk away, ¾ mile away and the 1 mile away. The sites belong to private landowners. The children walk to and from the site each session, building up to the longest distance as toddlers. The furthest site is a half-hour walk away. The adult to child ratio is 1:4 for children two years and above and this is maintained by staff. The setting has four Forest School leaders (Level 3) and two Forest School assistants (Level 2) across two nurseries and they work between both settings.

The nursery either follows the Montessori Curriculum for Life, an activity created in class (by children) or a particular child's need as the starting point for a Forest School related task. At the session the teacher introduces the starting point and children choose to stay with it or follow their own interests.

Friends Forest Nursery School, Surrey.

OUTSIDE HELP

Some schools/educational settings do not have trained Forest School leaders and rely on Independent leaders, wildlife trusts, park professionals, Environmental and Outdoor Learning Teams and Children's Services to help them deliver Forest School sessions.

Some local authorities and county councils have established 'Forest School Mentors' who support candidates undertaking Forest School training. The mentors have undertaken a formal induction process and provide an established Forest School programme which visitors can observe.

Local authorities and county councils may also have 'Borrow Boxes', whereby practitioners can borrow items for half a term.

Borrow Boxes may include the following:

- Presentation toolkits
- Outdoor clothing
- Tools
- Kelly Kettles
- Storm shelters
- Ropes and pulleys
- Den building materials.

Additional information and similarities concerning the case studies

All of the case studies reported using tools with children. The most commonly used tool was the vegetable peeler. This was used for whittling bark off sticks or for peeling vegetables and fruit for snack. Generally, Forest School leaders progressed on to challenging tools after adults were adequately trained and children had gained the necessary skills to be able to use the tools safely.

Each case study reported having a fire with the children, although the frequency of fires varied. Eastwood Nursery School have a fire in a fire pit or bowl and Randolph Beresford Nursery have a fire in a Kelly Kettle at least once during a block of sessions. Friends Forest Nursery School

PLANNING GUIDANCE

Ensure planning reflects the learner's age, stage of development and interests.

- Follow children's fascinations and explorations.

- Have high expectations of children. Believe in their competencies and abilities.

- Allow children to have plenty of autonomy and choice at Forest School.

- Plan tasks which are meaningful and relevant to children's lives (eg. this might involve learning how to tie knots/hitches, during a small achievable task, so they can make dens or a rope swing secure).

- Give children plenty of opportunities to practice skills they have learnt. They will need time to revisit, build on and consolidate experiences and learning.

- Put together resources or theme boxes to support fun outdoor learning.

- Make links to other areas in the curriculum, helping them to develop their thinking and understanding and construct new meanings.

- Offer appropriate space to encourage forms of phyical, social and emotional activity. It Is important that children feel a sense of space and security.

and Graffham Infants and Duncton CE Juniors Forest School use a fire during most sessions. In all cases, the children were introduced to fire maintenance and safety through discussion and games. Once the leaders felt the children were ready, fires were lit and used.

All of the case studies reported that children are encouraged to go to the toilet before they leave for Forest School. There are toilets available in the park and on the university campus; however, it was reported that in all of the case studies that generally children choose to go behind the privacy of a tree.

In most of the case studies, the boundaries on site are verbally agreed landmarks or marked by bows or boundary tape. Eastwood Nursery and Randolph Beresford Nursery allow venturing wherever their interests take them; however, the children must notify an adult when they wish to venture away from the group so that adults can maintain a suitable supervisory distance.

Planning for each session

The Foundation Stage curriculum guidance clearly states that practitioners need to be planning good quality learning experiences indoors and outdoors. In most settings staff collaboratively produce long-term and medium-term plans. In a Forest School context these plans will link to aspects of the EYFS and incorporate experiences afforded across seasons and weather.

There are obvious benefits to recording ideas, making links to learning, identifying key resources and vocabulary. Planning in advance can help you think in advance how you will effectively support, question and elicit as well as work through misconceptions, track experiences and assess children's learning. However, it is important that all plans are informed by observation, remain flexible and do not govern the session but rather complement it. Children's interests need to be followed, as they will learn more from play and learning experiences that are in context, meaningful and relevant to their lives. Planned activities should encourage independence, self-initiated and self-directed learning.

For example of a session plan for Eastwood Nursery School, see page 90.

Equal Opportunities and inclusion at Forest School

When developing a Forest School it is important to consider how it will be made inclusive for all participants (children, parents, helpers and staff).

Consideration needs to be given to the gender, cultural diversity, languages, special needs, ranges in ability and prior experience, and differing socio-economic backgrounds. By considering these, practitioners will be able to create an environment that supports everyone. Interestingly, there is no set ability groups at Forest School, children and staff are encouraged to learn from each other.

Children and adults may be hesitant or reluctant to participate. This is often influenced by their previous experience or lack of experience as well as their knowledge of the outdoors.

It is important to be understanding that some participants will need more support and encouragement than others and that for some entering natural spaces is not the norm, and therefore, can be uncomfortable.

Pairing children up with special friends can support less confident children or newcomers.

Some examples of how settings have made Forest School inclusive:

- Creating homemade books in children's home languages by using websites to translate simple text or by asking parent to record short simple sentences in their home language.

- Selecting stories about nature from other cultures, genres and in other languages.

- Incorporating songs, poetry and jokes about nature from other cultures.

- Encouraging children and parents to annotate photographs or drawings together.

- Creating audio books. Children could record a Forest School inspired story or share an experience with a practitioner or their parent.

- Creating photo albums of favourite photographs taken by the child and staff.

- Creating a world recipe book of foods made over fire or hot or cold drinks served from other cultures.

- Providing clothing and equipment for parents and staff who cannot afford to provide it.

- Adapting equipment, resources to simplify or set more challenging tasks.

- Making the Forest School site more assessable for children with mobility challenges.

- Creating visual time tables for children, this is particularly those who find transitions difficult. Many setting warn children in advance of transitions.

- By encouraging the participation of boys and girls, mothers and fathers.

- Adapting learning to suit learning styles and multiple intelligences

- By encouraging staff and children to work and play collaboratively.

- Find ways of incorporating British Sign Language (or Makaton) and visual prompts for children with communication and language difficulties.

What resources do you need?

Less emphasis on equipment and more focus on exploring natural objects will encourage more creative play. Adults may need to support children in the change of environment through role modelling how natural open-ended resources

- Emergency kit – includes a first aid kit stocked with items appropriate for the number of people out and the remoteness of the site, list of children with allergies and medication, risk assessments, wet wipes, bin bags, fire blanket, accident book and pen, spare clothes and scissors.

- Medications for children with allergies or illnesses. Medicines must be correctly labelled and be administered as outlined on the setting's medical form which has been completed by parents.

- Emergency procedures – for missing child, first aid, sudden inclement weather, sick child, allergic reactions.

- Mobile phone – contact numbers for the setting, colleagues and emergency numbers.

- Register, medical information, emergency contact details of all children and adults in the group.

- Clothing: The clothing required will depend on the weather. This may include protection from the sun (hats and sun cream), cold weather (e.g. hats, warm socks and mittens), or wet weather (e.g. waterproof clothing and footwear). Long-sleeved tops and trousers are recommended all time of year to protect children's arms and legs from the elements and from wildlife. Visibility vests may help make children more visible to motorists when they are crossing roads or to practitioners when they are in natural spaces.

- Be prepared for the occasional accident, pack spare socks, clothes, wipes and a plastic bag for soiled clothes.

- Clean water.

can be used in a variety of ways to support play and learning. Suggested below are some practical resources you will need to consider when planning for the groups' needs, safety, and planned activities:

- Trained Forest School leader – trained to Level 3 or higher.

- Adult helpers – research has suggested that it is good practice to have a ratio of one adult to every four children. This will help create an environment where children and adults feel supported in encouraging risk taking and following children's interests. Opportunities to follow children's lines of inquiry and share thinking are increased when ratios are high. All adults working with children will need vetted for suitability and have CRB clearance.

- Suitable site – permission granted and risk assessed.

- Transportation – to get to and from the site. Procedures will need to be in place for walking along and crossing busy roads, safety and seating plans for minibuses and carrying or transporting kit (such as tools and equipment).

- Lesson plan and risk assessments.

TOP TIP

Children can be encouraged to discuss the weather and suitable clothing. They can think about the types of play or activities they plan to be involved in and discuss and gather the resources needed for the session. Children can be encouraged to be responsible for looking after particular resources, especially if they have their own Forest School rucksack.

At Friends Forest Nursery children are responsible for ticking off the kit being packed into Forest School rucksacks.

Learning takes place when children are actively involved. The best Forest Schools environments encourage autonomy and emphasise process (at the learner's pace) rather than outcomes or targets. Understanding is a continual process and Forest School leaders facilitate appropriate and safe learning experiences which help children make new connections. In Danish Forest Schools, children often have free access to resources (such as tools and other equipment) in the base camp or in sheds. Adults are always on hand to support and supervise children using tools.

■ Drink and food may be prepared in advance or during the Forest School session (e.g. in the base camp or over a campfire).

☐ All food should be stored in airtight containers and only clean equipment should be used. Ensure food is prepared or cooked correctly. Be sure all equipment and waste is cleared away after use. Pay special attention to hygiene and children's dietary requirements. The amount of food and drink and equipment needed will depend on what is planned and the length of time spent outdoors. Before eating and drinking, antibacterial hand gel should be applied, particularly when washing hands with clean running water is not possible. It is good practice to pack a large bottle of water and cups for all sessions to keep children and adults hydrated. On day outings, children could be encouraged to pack healthy drinks and food from home. A cold drink is refreshing on hot days and a warm drink will help keep bodies warm when the weather is cold. Allowing children to help prepare the refreshments will support their understanding of hygiene, food preparation, quantities/amounts and looking after ourselves and others.

■ Ground sheet.

■ Roll mat and blanket.

■ Storm shelter and survival blankets/bags – in case the weather suddenly turns inclement.

■ Boundary tape or markers.

■ Portable potties and nappies (where necessary).

■ General resources: rucksack, books (fiction and non-fiction), tools, equipment, safety supplies (safety gloves), fire resources (including matches), camera, dictaphone, observation forms, clipboard and pen, collecting bags or containers. Some Forest Schools have separate rucksacks for emergency kit, equipment and tools, educational resources, snack and spare clothes. These bags are usually tagged for easy identification.

Resources are often found around the educational setting or in the natural environment. However, over time you may wish to purchase additional resources or invest in clothing or specialist equipment. Suppliers selling Forest School resources can be found by doing an online search for 'Forest School equipment and resources'.

Don't forget… to check your setting's insurance as there may be restrictions on tree climbing and tool use.

Supporting children in the environment

Bentsen et al. (2010) note that the Scandinavian concept of 'udeskole' (meaning outdoor school) is a learning approach

that 'emerged as a way to engage children with nature through educational concepts' (p.1).

The 'Early Years Outdoors Vision and Values for Outdoor Play' published by Learning Through Landscapes, describes in detail the visions and core values for high quality outdoor experiences. The vision for all young children states that:

'All children have the right to experience and enjoy the essential and special nature of being outdoors. Young children thrive and their minds and bodies develop best when they have free access to stimulating outdoor environments for learning through play and real experiences. Knowledgeable and enthusiastic adults are crucial to unlocking the potential of outdoors.'

(The full document can be accessed at: http://www.educationscotland.gov.uk/images/Vision_and_Values_for_Outdoor_Play_tcm4-597073.pdf)

We know that the natural world is stimulating and can engage all the senses. It's important that children have experience in a range of outdoor spaces (natural and created by main) as this will broaden their experiences and help them make new connections, furthering their understanding of outdoor environments.

The adult's function at Forest School will take on different roles at different times, for different children. There will be times where the adult is a facilitator, guide, model, boundary setter, negotiator, mediator, fellow investigator, inquirer, playmate, friend or comforter.

Gulløv (2003) a researcher who studied Danish Kindergartens states that in Danish outdoor schools (or 'udeskole') adults 'function as observers and promoters of different activities' and there is no pressure on the children to participate or 'any ideas expressed of the educational outcomes of the activities' (p.34). The pedagogical aim of udeskole, according to Gulløv is to teach children to make decisions and to take responsibility.

Ultimately, Forest School should aim to ensure learning is initiated by the children and not imposed on them by practitioners trying to meet curriculum targets.

Reflecting on and evaluating sessions

When reflecting with children, it is important to reflect on your own talk. Is there a balance between your talk and that of the children? How do you show the children that you are listening and that their contributions are valued?

We want children to be able to identify what they can do and what they want to be able to do. This will help them identify what they need to learn to achieve their goal.

For example, a child wanting to build a tyre swing may be able to identify the resources needed; however, they might need to learn which rope will be suitable and which knots are required to safely secure the rope to the tyre and to the tree. During a reflection session, children may discuss what they did, how the session went, what they liked, what they did not like, the resources needed for the next session as well as what they have learnt and what they would like to learn next.

It's important that practitioners share their reflections with the children and what they are learning as it models language and shows that reflection and learning is an ongoing process, even in adulthood. Adults do not always know the answers to questions. Practitioners can discuss with children where we might find out the answer to their questions, using a variety of sources (such as through investigation, books, internet searches, asking other children, staff, parents and occasionally 'experts').

CASE STUDY: REFLECTION TREES

The children found a large tree branch that resembled a small tree. A group of children carried it back to the setting and it was transformed into a 'Reflection Tree'. After each session, the children and adults discuss what they liked, disliked or learnt at Forest School. The adults support recording the children's ideas onto a paper leaf. The children then attach the leaf with string or wire to the tree.

Find out from the council when park rangers and tree surgeons will be working in your area as this may give you an opportunity to acquire parts of trees (eg. branches or logs) which could be useful for indoor or outdoor activities back at your setting.

Eastwood Nursery School Centre for Children and Families, Borough of Wandsworth, London.

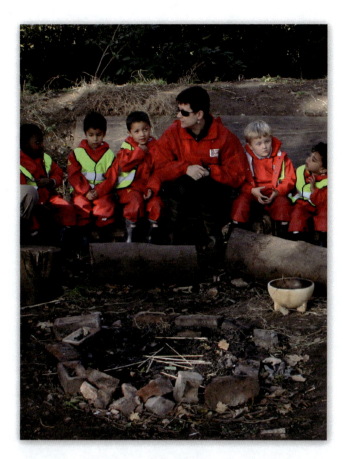

REFLECTION: BEST PRACTICE

Chelsea Open Air Nursery School and Children's Centre, London, encourages parents to share with staff how they think Forest School has helped their child. Below is a quote from a parent:

"I really am amazed at the change in M, I was having a really tough time getting her to school every morning, we had tears and tantrums every day for months it seemed, refusing to get dressed, getting out of the buggy and running in the opposite direction from school, screaming outside the nursery that she didn't want to go in. I found it really hard, but we seem to have come through it, I think Forest School has been great for forming friendships for her and boosting her confidence and it really is such a relief for me and a weight off of my shoulders which I am sure she could sense even though I tried hard not to show it to her. Thank you, N."

Educationalists need to explore how to best utilise outdoor spaces in an educational context. It is important that children are given the opportunity to visit a range of outdoor spaces so that they can discover the opportunities each space affords. We know that children value outdoor spaces and for many it is their preferred environment at nursery.

By consulting and listening to children, practitioners can gain a deeper understanding of the importance of outdoors spaces. The information gathered can be used to support children's play, education and development. Practitioners can help children develop their emotional vocabulary by facilitating time within a session for children to focus on self-reflection, assessment and evaluation. Reflection activities allow children to review and discuss parts of the session, their feelings, their difficulties, and their responses. They will be able to find ways to face challenge, make improvements and solve problems by developing their analytical skills and constructive thinking.

Reflection – examples from practice

Children and adults at Friends Forest Nursery in Surrey hold a celebration of learning at the end of each session, whereby adults and children share what they did, what they enjoyed and did not enjoy. When the children have returned to the setting they bring their experiences to the feedback table so that they can share with parents, the objects found, items made as well as video or photographs taken during the session.

At Randolph Beresford Centre, staff have noticed the children are very tired at the end of the session. Some children need time and space before they are ready to reflect, whereas others are happy to reflect at the end of the session. The children who choose to reflect at the end of a lesson will revisit experiences from the session and look at what they have collected.

Graffham Infants and Duncton CE Juniors Forest School reflect during the session as well as hold an end of session discussion. These discussions often continue in class and encourage the children to be open about the skills that they are developing (e.g. leadership).

At the end of a block of sessions Eastwood Nursery School invites parents to watch a slide show featuring photos children have chosen to share. The photos represent the children's experience and shares what they have been learning or exploring through play and small achievable tasks.

More ideas to support reflection are discussed in the **Elicitation and questioning** and the **Documentation** sections.

EXAMPLE OF BEST PRACTICE

Floorbooks are books made out of large sheets of paper. The book is made by a group with an adult or child writing individual's words, ideas, predictions and questions exactly as worded on the paper.

Claire Warden of Mindstretchers in Scotland developed 'Talking and Thinking Floorbooks' – an adaptation of floorbooks. These encourage thinking skills through group consultation and exploratory talk so that children can influence the learning taking place.

(To find out more about 'Taking and Thinking Books' visit http://www.mindstretchers.co.uk/articles/floorbooks.html)

Elicitation and questioning

Children are naturally curious about their environment. Inquiry involves investigating, asking questions, exploring and examining.

Elicitation is a process of discovering and clarifying children's existing ideas which have been developed from experience and interaction with others. It can give the practitioner useful insight into children's current understanding of concepts and inform the support offered by the adult or peers. It can help the practitioner identify children's misconceptions and provide a platform for investigation and clarification through additional support or extension activities.

The elicitation process involves observing a child. This is followed by questioning. Questioning is not an easy task and research suggests that even in the best educational setting, practitioners find the process of asking effective questions challenging. Effective questioning is developed with experience, professional development and practice. To be effective, questions need to be carefully targeted, meaningful, and relevant and age appropriate. Effective questioning will engage children's minds and develop their understanding. This is achieved in an environment where children feel their contributions are valued, where they are active participants, able to investigate and explore their ideas or interests.

Children develop language at different rates; their range of language will be dependent on their experience and exposure to vocabulary.

It's important to remember that children do not necessarily ask questions verbally. Practitioners need to be skilled observers to be able to identify the types of questions or concepts children are exploring through play. The adults who model asking questions will help children develop their own questioning skills. Generally as children get older, they start to answer more complex and abstract questions.

There are five main question words: *Who/What/Where/Why/How* and children tend to understand these in that order. 'How' questions can be difficult for young children as they involve reasoning. Visual aids such as photographs or artefacts may support children to develop reasoning skills.

Questions should be as open as possible so that they create opportunities for discussion. There will be times when closed questions are appropriate (e.g. those requiring a yes or no or one word answers).

Here are some examples of questions:

- Why do you think that happened?

- What do you think of...?

- How is it different from...?

- What has changed...?

- Jayden thought... what do you think?

- How did you do that?

- Why did you...?

- Can you tell me about...?

- I wonder what would happen if...?

- I wonder why...

- I wonder how...?

- Can you guess...?

Finding out and recording children's existing ideas can be achieved through various elicitation strategies either at Forest School or back in educational settings.

Some popular methods include: annotated drawings, concept mapping, sorting their natural collections and floorbooks. Children and adults work collaboratively in these activities and share ideas and experiences, explore concepts through talk, providing a rich learning environment.

Recording children's existing ideas, their predictions/hypotheses can help practitioners clearly identify changes between what children knew about a concept before as opposed to after further experience, exploration and talk. The process helps everyone reflect on the learning which has occurred.

When reflecting on learning we can look at changes in behaviour and feelings as well as new perspectives, ideas and understanding of concepts. It can support children in being able to self-assess their own learning, as well as make peer assessments.

Ways to reflect with children and adults

Reflecting and following-up on sessions is an important and personalised part of each Forest School experience.

Incorporating time to reflect into sessions is not always easy, particularly when time is limited. Just as some adults find the process of reflection difficult, so will children.

Some children will be keen to share what they did or saw, providing incentive for follow-up work. Others will need longer to think about their experience before they are ready to produce something related to it. Children's minds will be occupied with sensory feedback. There is also a lot of information being processed as a result of so many areas of the brain being activated.

Children and adults will be attracted to different aspects and elements from the environment. They will also have preferred ways of communicating their thoughts, feelings and ideas. By offering a variety of materials and methods practitioners can identify children's preferred ways of communicating and support children in retracing steps, reflecting on learning and development and identifying key aspects and areas of interest. Materials and resources aimed at promoting reflection should be available back in the setting so that children can access these freely, when they are ready. Practitioners have helped children recall and reflect on their Forest School experiences through:

- Encouraging children to collect artefacts.

- Photography.

- Video recordings.

- Making books or displays.

- Writing down children's thoughts, comments and questions in the child's words.

- Encouraging children to write or make marks.

- Creating digital diaries or slideshows of photographs.

- Placing objects under a visualizers and digital microscope or on a light trolley.

- Creating an interest tables.

- Putting together collections of objects.

- Recording children's voices on recordable devices.

- Drawing and painting.

- Making models.

- Creating small world scenes of Forest School or of Forest School experiences.

- Providing a range of books fiction and non-fiction for children to refer to.

Documentation

Documentation provides a written or pictorial record of what has occurred and providing a visible account of a child's learning journey. The gathering and organisation of the information gathered provides a record of significant learning and can help practitioners plan learning experiences and devise goals for individual children or a group to support children's development. It also can be used as a way of aiding children's metacognition as they revisit, reflect on and enrich their understanding of their learning and the learning environment.

Documentation can be gathered through many ways such as through observation, photographs, video or audio recording, transcribing children's comments, practitioner observations and collecting pieces of work.

Staff need to consider when it is appropriate to document children's learning. Documentation should highlight significant learning and experiences for a child. In deciding what is significant, practitioners may need to have conversations with colleagues, parents and indeed the children. They will need to explore what the child was learning during an experience, the effort a child has put into a task and the child's involvement or engagement levels during the process.

Described below are creative ways settings are documenting significant experiences and learning from children's Forest School sessions.

Creative documentation guidance

- Photo albums with recordable pages – recording sound clips corresponding to photographs in the book.

- Displays – showing the children's drawings, paintings, constructions, art, photographs, artefacts and comments.

- Digital photo frames – showing photographs for children and families.

- Handmade books or stories made in the setting about their experiences – children can be encouraged to record their experiences either in writing or in audio with the help of a practitioner or parent.

- Handmade books to take home can contain photos, artefacts (of objects collected) and drawings to help memory and stimulate conversation between children and their parents.

- Parent comment books – where parents can leave comments about what the children have told them at home. Parents can also make comments in children's documentation books.

Knowledge and skills

The knowledge and skills of practitioners working with young children can have a significant impact on children's development. Defries (2009) highlights that: *'practitioners' lack of understanding of outdoor play emerged as the biggest barrier'* to developing better outdoor learning provision. Effective education strongly depends on practitioners' willingness to improve their own practice and their motivation to improve standards for children. Children, Schools and Families Committee (2010) and Ofsted (2008) highlight that more professional learning and new approaches to teaching can support change and improve children's access to learning beyond the educational setting.

To set up a successful Forest School, you must really have a desire and commitment to do it. It should not be treated as an educational fad but instead be an integral part of the total philosophy of a setting.

Formal training is advisable as it is different from outdoor learning, which has become common practice in educational settings.

Carrying out action research in your setting is an effective way of becoming a reflective practitioner. Having time to learn and apply new theories, network and discuss ideas with other professionals will help you see your practice and provision in new ways, helping you to identify what you are doing well and where improvements can be made.

Seeing children as co-constructors of their environment

Young children are well placed to advise adults on their learning environments. We can learn a lot by observing children's play outside and by asking older children to describe what they enjoy doing as well as what do not like or what they wish they could do.

All children need to understand that they have rights. For example, the right to a safe and stimulating environment, to have their opinions and perspectives respected.

With rights come responsibilities and as adults we need to help children understand the rights of others. Children should feel they have the power to be autonomous, make decisions, follow their lines of inquiry and take risks but may need help in understanding that from time to time we need to collaborate, compromise and negotiate to meet the needs of a larger group.

TOP TIP: PLANNING

A good starting point when planning for outdoor experiences is to ask the adults to revert to their own childhood, recalling the activities they enjoyed doing with friends and family outdoors.

Practitioners at outdoor play conferences have recalled memories of playing freely in natural spaces such as woods, fields, orchards, gardens, parks, streams, beaches, moors, caves as well as man-made spaces such farms as quarries, canals bomb sites, in the street or back lane and even 'soot' pits. Some of the most memorable activities in these areas included special people, risk or challenge, physical activity, movement (eg. running, cycling, climbing, jumping or swinging), role or pretend play (eg. superhero play, dressing up, making dens, homes for elves, making mud pies or perfume), social play (eg. games such as chase, rounders, conkers, hide and seek or group picnics or campfires) or the exploration of the natural features such as plants (eg. hiding in trees or long grass, collecting leaves and conkers or pressing flowers) or animals (eg. collecting insects, frog spawn or catching newts or fish, pond dipping, rock pooling).

When given opportunities to express their perspectives, they can alter our thoughts and bring about substantial change. Enriched learning environments outside of classrooms have the power to not only stimulate and motivate children but also the adults working with them.

Forest School and Every Child Matters

Forest School links to the five outcomes of the 'Every Child Matters' framework and with various initiatives such as Rights Respecting Schools Award (UNICEF), Healthy Schools status, Sustainable Schools and Eco Schools.

The 'Every Child Matters' (ECM) framework identifies the five outcomes that are most important to children and young people. The five outcomes are universal ambitions for every child and young person, whatever their background or circumstances. Improving outcomes for all children and young people underpins all of the development and work within children's trusts.

Researchers O'Brien and Murray (2006) believe that 'Forest School can contribute to four out of five outcomes…' (p.6). Although the fifth outcome is difficult to measure and requires longitudinal studies to be carried out, we can speculate how Forest School may help children achieve economic well-being.

The Forest School programme at Eastwood Nursery School Centre for Children and Families clearly links to this document.

The five outcomes are:

- Be healthy

- Stay safe

- Enjoy and achieve

- Make a positive contribution

- Achieve economic well-being.

Be healthy

- Mentally and emotionally healthy

- Physically healthy and adopt healthy lifestyles.

Children are generally physically active at Forest School and as they continue through sessions will build their strength and stamina. Their experience can encourage them to adopt healthier lifestyles in and outside the educational setting. Positive outdoor experiences may be transferred to the home environment as children encourage their parents to take them out to woodland, parks or other green spaces. The natural outdoor spaces can help reduce stress levels by having a calming and beneficial effect on children and adults alike. Open outdoor spaces give children a sense of freedom. Fresh clean air can make people feel more alert. Through repeated exposure there are likely to be improvements to confidence and self-esteem, which positively link to emotional and mental well-being.

Natural environments can be more accommodating than indoor and outdoor spaces in educational settings. Natural environments offer places for children to be quiet and out of direct view as well as be loud and adventurous.

Stay safe

- Safe from accidental injury or death

- Have security, stability and are cared for.

The 'wild', and yet controlled, safe environment of Forest School encourages children to quickly learn to self-assess risk by making sensible and informed decisions. With increasing familiarity, they test their boundaries, learn what is safe and explore ways of dealing with unfamiliar and unpredictable situations. Much of the learning come from opportunities children have for testing their knowledge, skills and abilities in a real-life context.

Enjoy and achieve

- Achieve stretching national educational standards at primary school

- Achieve personal and social development and enjoy recreation.

Forest School offers a change in learning context. Within this context children can undertake a range of practical activities and carry out small achievable tasks not necessarily available in the educational setting. Learning opportunities outdoors may be greater than those achievable indoors, linking to all areas of the early years and primary curriculums.

Green outdoor spaces contain open-ended natural resources with open-ended possibilities which promote creative thinking.

At Forest School, children make new connections to build on their existing experience and knowledge and skills. They have opportunities to work collaboratively as well as discover ways of becoming more independent.

Those who are unfamiliar with woodlands and green spaces can become confident in using them, potentially spurring a life-long relationship with natural spaces.

Making a positive contribution

- Develop self confidence and successfully deal with significant life changes and challenges

- Developing enterprising behaviour.

Children develop confidence and self control as they become familiar with the Forest School environment. Their confidence may be transferred to the educational setting and into other areas of their lives.

Forest School incorporates all learning styles and intelligences and can be particularly effective for children who do not do well in the classroom environment. Children learn to solve problems, be creative and imaginative at Forest School, thus showing enterprising behaviour.

Achieve economic well-being

- Helping learners to envisage a positive future for themselves and their families.

Forest School helps children understand the importance of being healthy and respecting the environment for future generations. Through having direct contact with nature, children become aware of the wonders of nature, relate to natural areas in their local community and develop personal morality towards them. Having regular exposure to a variety of outdoor spaces will help dispel myths and reduce fear factors associated with them. In the future, this may help them be responsible citizens, encouraging them to make positive health and environmental choices for themselves and their families. It also encourages children and families to think about free or low cost outdoor activities available in their community for relaxation and recreation.

In today's environmental climate, it has never been more essential to highlight the importance of conservation. The truth is, we cannot afford to disinherit ourselves or our children from nature nor can we ignore the lack of respect for the natural environment. The consequences of our past and present lifestyle are evident with the myriad of human inflicted environmental disasters. Children need help in understanding their role in looking after the planet now and for future generations.

Making Forest School multicultural

Incorporating aspects of the cultural backgrounds of the children, families and staff in your setting is an effective way to ensure everyone feels they are valued and have something to contribute. Celebrating diversity at Forest School will help children learn about the multicultural and ethnically diverse world we live in.

Use the cultural resource base in your setting to enhance the provision. Encourage children, parents, staff, grandparents to share aspects of their cultural background through activities offered at Forest School.

These might involve sharing:

- Ways of preparing foods over a campfire

- Language, songs, poetry, stories, folklore, mythology or legends

- Outdoor festivals, dances, music, sports, social gatherings and ceremonies performed outdoors

- Photographs of homes and dwellings in other countries.

Chapter 4: Forest School and activities for children

Getting children on board

Although there is a lot of research highlighting children's preferences to playing and learning in outdoor environments, feeling comfortable in natural spaces may not come naturally to all children. There may be children in a setting who are reluctant to take part in Forest School. Practitioners should try to find out why the child does not want to participate and support them.

Forest School leaders have reported children not wanting to participate in Forest School for the following reasons:

- The child does not want to leave a special adult, friend or object at nursery.

- The child does not want to get dressed in the waterproof suits or wellies.

- The child does not understand where he or she is going.

With careful consideration to the children's needs, practitioners can help the child overcome most of their anxieties associated with participating.

Offering progressions

Personalised learning involves planning for each child. Before embarking on the first Forest School outing, observe

what children are enjoying doing in the setting. If you are a freelance Forest School leader, arrange time to observe the children or speak to staff from the setting about what the children can do and enjoy doing. Find ways of incorporating these activities into Forest School sessions.

Children develop in individual ways and rates and may need to gradually build up their time spent outdoors in natural settings away from the usual early years setting.

Some children may not know what to do when they are at Forest School. They may not be accustomed to play in natural spaces with natural objects. It is important that Forest School leaders have ideas or planned activities in mind to encourage children to get involved. It is important that all planned activities are flexible and can be adapted where necessary. There should be a gradual transition away from adult-led activities to those which are child-led.

Clothing for children and adults

'There is no such thing as inappropriate weather, just inappropriate clothing' and perhaps, an inappropriate attitude. Appropriate clothing will help make the session safe and enjoyable for all.

Some settings have opted to buy waterproofs for the children and staff to use on Forest School settings. This is beneficial because:

- Children and adults will not feel under pressure to keep their own clothes clean

- There is no excuse for not participating because the clothing is available onsite

- Everyone will have the same kit and this will help children and adults identify who is in their group.

Most of the year the children can wear waterproof suits. Most three- to five-year-olds prefer waterproof dungarees and coats. There are a range of suppliers available on the Internet by searching 'children's waterproofs'.

Babies and toddlers can either wear in all-in-one piece suits (which tend to be warmer in the winter months as there are less places for heat to escape) or dungarees and coats.

When purchasing waterproofs, it is important to think about colour, what will be highly visible in the environment, what colours children will prefer to wear, what will wear well over the course of a few seasons. Ensure they are easy to wash. No-one will want to wear a soiled suit. Light-coloured waterproofs will show stains more than dark colours. Although there may be standard sizing for age groups, you may need to buy a few suits outside the age range to cater for the children in your group.

- Children's high-visibility vests are recommended for children travelling along roads and those using public areas.

- Children can be encouraged to bring in their own wellington boots; however, it is a good idea to have some pairs available for children to borrow in case they are forgotten at home.

- Child-sized rucksacks are great for holding water bottles, snacks, lunches and equipment the child may want to bring out with them. On occasion, they may also serve to hold that special toy from home which the child does not want to leave behind at nursery.

During winter months, children can wear layers of warm clothing under their waterproofs; they should also wear thick socks (or several pairs of socks) in the wellies and a hat. It is advisable to purchase waterproof mittens for children to place over their hands as they get cold very quickly.

Before purchasing waterproofs, try and involve the children in the decision. Staff at Eastwood Nursery School consulted the children on their favourite colours of dungarees and coats from a catalogue. They discovered that red was the colour most children preferred. The staff purchased red coats and waterproof trousers so they were dressed similar to the children. Eastwood Nursery found that with everyone wearing the same kit, potential issues of inequality (and arguments over kit) were prevented. The adults wearing similar kit to the children were in a good position to model what to wear and how to get dressed.

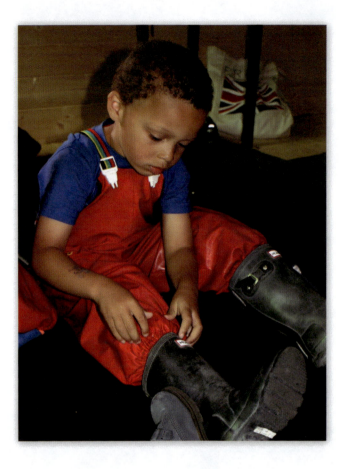

On dry summer days, children should be able to get away with long-sleeved cotton tops and trousers. It is important that the child's legs and arms are covered to prevent scratches, stings and bites. It also helps protect the skin from the sun. Summer footwear should be comfortable, sturdy and closed toe to prevent accidents.

Consider packing spare clothing and footwear, in event of an accident outdoors. Forest School leaders often find that spare socks are most often needed, particularly after children have been jumping in puddles or mud.

Getting ready and undressed independently

Getting ready is an important part of the Forest School experience, children need to be allowed as much time as necessary to get ready independently, even if it takes the whole session. Allowing children space and time to get ready at their own pace will develop autonomy, confidence and skills.

There are plenty of opportunity for learning, discussing weather and suitable clothing, selecting appropriate sizes of clothing and boots and helping each other.

Some children will be able to get dressed independently, while others will need additional support.

Adults can support children getting dressed independently by:

- Using adults or other children to demonstrate getting dressed and modelling language.

- Providing visual routines and photographs showing the sequence in which clothing is put on.

- Using a puppet, soft toy, or adult to make a deliberate mistake and asking the children to offer suggestions to rectify the situation.

- Encouraging children to ask other children and adults for help.

- Making suggestions of child helpers or assigning buddies to support those who are struggling to get dressed.

- Singing a song to help them get dressed 'this is the way we put on our (dungarees, coats, and boots)…when we get dressed for Forest School' (To the tune of: 'Here we go round the mulberry bush').

- Playing games such as setting a timer to see how long it takes a group to get ready (once the children know how) and seeing if the group can be beat the time next session.

Children and adults should discuss planned activities as well as activities suggested by children on the day. They will need to consider what resources they will need to bring with them. Forest School can be done without expensive equipment and resources. The essential resources to consider when planning sessions were described in Chapter 3. However, here are some additional ideas for a basic kit to support play and activity in the natural environment.

- Bug pots and magnifiers

- Ropes and string

- Pulleys

- Den building materials (tarpaulins of various sizes, fabrics or old bed sheets)

- Clothing pegs, tent pegs, and mallets

- Tools

- Poles

- Baskets and bags for collecting

- Buckets and wooden spoons.

Children enjoy being responsible for packing these items and carrying them in a rucksack. They may need to be reminded that they will be responsible for their rucksack and should therefore pack light. Heavy items should be discussed, assessing the needs of the group and upon agreement, given to adults to carry. It is also important that children are involved in thinking about the items that need to be taken out to help keep themselves and others safe at Forest School. This will involve discussing items such as high visibility vests, safety gloves, first aid kit, personal medications, mobile phones, emergency contact numbers and counting how many children and adults are in the group before going out, while on site and before leaving Forest School.

The same guidelines apply to getting undressed. It is important that children find it easy to find items and put them away.

Adults can support children finding clothing and equipment by:

- Clearly marking boxes for small, medium and large dungarees and coats. The clothing can also be marked inside the garments with small, medium or large, depending on the size.

- Marking sizes on the backs of wellington boots so children can find their size and attempt to order them.

- Clearly labelling storage for equipment. Photographs and labels, numbers or silhouettes of where equipment belongs will support learning and help foster independence when getting ready or putting away.

- Asking children to assign adults to tidy a certain area and choosing a set number of children to help. This will empower the children and ensure everyone works as a team to get tidied up.

The Early Years Foundation Stage

Forest School encourages development across all areas of the Early Years Foundation Stage (EYFS). However, international research has shown Forest School to be particularly effective in supporting the **prime** areas; Personal Social and Emotional Development; Communication and Language; and Physical Development.

TOP TIP

Adults can support children by:

- Giving them ample time and the necessary resources to explore independently.

- Acting as a fellow investigator and joining children in their discoveries.

- Posing questions to stimulate higher-level thinking.

- Sharing children's interests through documentation with key persons and parents.

- Extending the children's interests through planned activities in the early years setting or at home.

- Encouraging children to reflect on their experiences and share their likes and dislikes.

- Providing children with an increasing range of words to describe what they are doing and seeing.

- Encouraging children to think about safety and hygiene without limiting their experiences. This can include getting children to assess risks in advance of planned and spontaneous activities which may arise during a session.

Forest School is a multi-sensory environment offering children a world of learning opportunities through another context. Children can learn to make decisions, take risks, and solve problems.

Children need experiences of moving on a variety of natural surfaces. Some children may become fearful on surfaces that are not man-made, while others will enjoy rolling around on grass and in leaves. These experiences will enhance children's confidence in a broad range of environments while improving their balance and coordination.

There will be ample opportunity for children and adults to become deeply involved in natural phenomenon, both usual and unusual, but how these experiences are developed will depend on how tuned-in adults are to children's interests and lines of enquiry.

Children need ample time at Forest School to investigate the environment, this includes free uninterrupted time to play, as well as time to explore and make new connections through active learning, creating and thinking critically alongside peers and adults.

Practitioners will need to facilitate reasonable risks while remembering that young children will require close but non-intrusive observation and supervision. Risk-assessing involves assessing the risk benefits. We can always think of lots of reasons why we should not to do something – but it's equally important to consider why we should do it. Experience, training, and engaging in reflective dialogue with colleagues will help you plan enabling environments for children.

Children who enjoy throwing objects, rolling, climbing, running up/down gradients, swinging, hanging, off objects, seeing objects fall or being dropped into something else, jumping off or falling on or into something will benefit physically and cognitively from their experiments with gravity and force. These are important experiences that most children need and will actively seek out. It is important that practitioners consider the risks involved in such activities without unreasonably limiting them.

With the youngest children it is important to consider risks associated with objects being eaten, put up noses or being dropped on body parts. These risks can be mitigated through effective practice.

Ways in which Forest School supports the **prime** areas of the EYFS

Personal Social and Emotional Development:
Opportunities at Forest School will develop children's interests, attitudes and aesthetic awareness of the wider world. Children gain confidence by acquiring knowledge and skills and showing pride in achievement. There will be opportunities to try new activities, take risks when they are ready. There are opportunities for developing social skills through teamwork and helping peers. Children can develop their understanding of boundaries which promote safety and positive behaviour as well as risks.

Children learn independence through getting dressed and packed for Forest School. Once on site they can be

control and strength in their wrists by using tools, picking up and carrying objects and drawing and painting with natural objects and pigments. They will be able to gain an understanding of the effects different environments have on movement and how the mind and body can develop skills to adapt through practice and perseverance. Through movement opportunities children will develop an awareness of space. Tracking skills are developed, encouraging the children to use their body to slide, crawl and roll.

Ways in which Forest School supports the **specific** areas of the EYFS

Literacy: Children will have opportunities to identify print in the environment. They will be able to develop mark making and writing skills with mud or dirt with sticks or feathers. Songs, rhymes and poems, fiction and non-fiction books, and oral storytelling of familiar tales are excellent resources to develop language and literacy and can be linked to experiences or things found in the natural environment. Children can be involved in finding ways to record learning in documentation books or displays.

Mathematics: Children will have opportunities for matching colours and sorting natural materials according to various criteria. There are opportunities for counting and calculating, exploring patterns, shape and space in the natural environment. Children can explore concepts such as measurement by comparing length, height, size, capacity and weight of objects. This can be achieved through practical activities such as den building, cooking, collecting kindling and sticks for a fire or though imaginative play. Children can learn about keeping track of time through routines and cooking activities. Forest School encourages the use of positional and descriptive language.

Understanding the World: Children will have opportunities to find out and identify living things. They will show curiosity by talking and asking questions about what is seen and what is happening. They will develop an enquiry mind through making predictions, discussing past events, recording time and sequences, finding out how things work. Through observing and exploring they will be able to appreciate patterns and relationships, show an awareness of similarities, differences and change. There will be opportunities for children to plan activities and construct

encouraged to select resources independently. Children can learn ways to conserve, and protect nature, keep the environment clean. They will learn about how to maintain hygiene outdoors. The very active nature of Forest School releases 'feel good' chemicals in the brain which help promote a sense of emotional well-being.

Communication and Language: Children will broaden their vocabulary and develop listening skills in one-to-one and group contexts. They will develop conversational skills in practical ways. Children will be able to demonstrate how they are able to maintain concentration and involvement and make meaningful connections. They will use verbal and non-verbal communication to express feelings, needs, and thoughts and to think through problems. Asking, devising experiments and finding out answers concerned with the environment will develop thinking and enquiry approaches to learning.

Physical Development: Children build their strength by negotiating tricky terrain, climbing trees, getting in and out of ditches, moving logs, jumping, walking, running and rolling down grass hills. They can explore pushing and pulling movements through transporting objects, using ropes, pulleys and levers. Children will develop fine motor using real tools and equipment. There is scope for ICT (for example, digital cameras, video, audio recording devices and digital microscopes) to support investigation and documentation of learning.

Expressive arts and design: The natural environment fosters opportunities for children to explore colours and texture. There are opportunities for music making, sketching, nature rubbings, imaginative play, and creative storytelling. Children will be able to make representations, models and constructions using a range of mediums, natural materials and tools. Children can be involved in creating slide shows and talking photo albums using computer software to share their experiences with peers or parents.

Children under three and Forest School

Involving babies in Forest School will offer them a wider variety of experience. The environment promotes the use of all the senses, encouraging interest and learning in the world around them.

When working with under-threes it is important to allow plenty of time for exploration. What might seem insignificant to us can be of great interest to young children. All those things adults fail to notice now or have long forgotten, they are just discovering and trying to make sense of.

Offer children plenty of time to relish in discovering the world around them through uninterrupted play and adult support which is sensitive and individualized. They will respond to sensitive caregiving which is built on an understanding of their needs and is focused on building secure attachments.

Children under three-years-old are gaining increasing control of their bodies and movements. They will need opportunities to be mobile on a variety of surfaces and to be able to handle and manipulate objects. For children who are less mobile, you will need to bring objects to them by placing them in a basket or within in distance of them to move towards. Carefully check the objects for dangers before allowing the children to play with them. If you are not sure of the suitability of an object, do not offer it.

During the first three years, social, language and communication skills are developing quickly. To support these areas of development, children will need encouragement and ample interaction with peers and carers.

Below are examples of what you might experience children doing at different ages and stages of development and how you can plan opportunities to support them.

Birth-to-11 months

Children at this age are:

- Interested in sights, smells, sounds

- Turning to and looking at what they hear/are interested in

- Showing emotions shown through movements of fingers, arms and bodies

- Exploring through senses and examining texture and sensation: Objects such as moss, feathers, wood, stones, soil, and scented flowers will explore things through body movements, with hands and mouth

- Needing close contact and support of key persons.

- Enjoying being active through crawling, shuffling or walking

- Spending time observing and examining objects thoroughly using their senses

- Demonstrating personal interests and use of new vocabulary through emerging language and utterances.

They need opportunities to:

- Touch plants, objects

- Built up and knock down natural resources

- Play social games like peek-a-boo

- Collect and explore natural objects in baskets/containers (explore texture, weight and size)

- Listen for sounds and repeat them

- Join in songs or rhymes with actions and key vocabulary

- Find out about what are they seeing, hearing and doing with the language input from adults.

16-26 months

Children at this age are:

- Developing a curiosity about things and processes and will become absorbed when investigating

- Making more choices, develop confidence in their ability

They need opportunities to:

- Have close, meaningful adult contact

- Observe and explore the natural world. In a safe environment. Ensure objects provided are not harmful

- Be on the ground or on a blanket or ground sheet

- Have objects brought to them and some left at arm's length or hanging to encourage reaching movement

- Learn and use key words in English and home language

- Explore treasure baskets containing natural resources.

8-20 months

Children at this age are:

- Beginning to find out about the environment, their likes and dislikes and what it has to offer them

- Increasingly becoming more mobile and exploratory

TOP TIP

Space and a variety of ground cover and terrain help children to build their experience, confidence, balance, coordination and awareness of their body. Provide low-level stumps to encourage babies to pull themselves up to a standing position. Slopes and hills to climb up and down challenge children to explore and feel the effects gravity on their bodies. They are also learning where and when to start, change speed and stop.

- Generally have little sense of danger or awareness of hygiene issues. With adult support, they can begin to accept that some objects should not be touched

- Taking pleasure in revisiting familiar experiences as well as being intrigued by new ones.

They need opportunities to:

- Experiment, combine and manipulate materials, such as sand or soil and water, including adding natural objects to dough or soft clay

- 'Transport'/carry objects from one place to another

- Sort/match/fill/empty objects in baskets and different shaped and sized containers

- Use counting words

- Use single-word and two-word utterances

- Explore positional/action words: up, down, jumping in a meaningful context

- Push/pull (wagon, small log tied to a rope, rolling logs down a slope)

- Build small structures with natural materials

- Hide (e.g. in tee-pee/tent/natural structure)

- Explore plants, trees, surfaces, and puddles

- Develop independence, a sense of time and routine through practical activities such as: toileting, getting dressed, play, personal hygiene, snack time.

22-36 months

Children at this age are:

- Learning to make decisions based on preferences, interests and experience solve problems and grow in their confidence in their own abilities

- Showing more awareness to be able to recognise and respond to danger

CASE STUDY: BRINGING OUTSIDE INTERESTS IN

Gaby* was at Forest School on a wet day and discovered a puddle.

Staff carefully observed her actions. Gaby initially stared at the puddle and then started picking up handfuls of gravel and tossing them in. She watched the reaction the gravel had on the puddle, the splash and how the water changed colour. She repeated this behaviour several times, completely absorbed in what she was doing. Then, Gaby put both of her hands into the puddle and splashed the water and stirred it up with the palms of her hands. She had transformed the clear puddle into a murky one. Staff were able to link Gaby's actions to other behaviour linked to her interest in change and transforming objects back at Nursery. (*child's name has been changed)

- Showing stronger capability and interest towards self-care

- Seeking out others to share experiences

- Becoming more sociable in their play

- Exploring through systems of representation and symbolic representation.

They will need opportunities to:

- Investigate their outdoor environment purposefully and observe seasonal changes

- Test /experiment with their ideas predictions/theories

- Think through what they might need to wear outdoors, given the weather. Carry personal items in a backpack

- Problem-solve and collaborate

- Engage in imaginary play (making Forest School soup), building dens

- Explore movement, navigating obstacles and uneven terrain

- Play games such as hide and seek, 'One, two, three, where are you?' and those involving moving and freezing

PRACTICAL ACTIVITIES FOR OVER-3s

- Using natural objects to explore sound or make instruments

- Minibeast hunt

- Texture hunt

- Matching natural objects to colour paint swatches

- Bird watching

- Animal homes

- Leaf/bark rubbings

- Recording bird calls

- Building a rope swing

- Constructing a stick man/woman

- Making a hat

- Story rope or a story stick

- Willow wands

- Leaf pit

- Making Forest School soup

- Constructing a pulley system using ropes

- Camouflage clothes and paints

- Looking for and making moulds of animal tracks

- Painting with natural pigments

- Making kites

- Light and shadows

- Creating natural collages

- Reflections such as those in water or using mirrors to look into tree canopy

- Whittling elder

- Making perfume

- Weaving grasses

- Making a walking stick

- Making a story stick

- Making a mobile

- Creating sculptures

- Using tools loppers, bow saws, tenon saws, hammer and nails

- Playing games such as hide and seek safety game

- Sketching

- Lighting a fire and cooking

- Going on a shape hunt

- Making feely bags

- Collecting objects in bags and sorting them

- Making a map – to be used to show a peer how to get to a secret place or to help locate hidden treasure or buried acorns.

- Playing social games such as 'hide and seek', and 'duck, duck, goose' (which can be adapted to include woodland animals)

- Creating mud kitchens

- Tying knots

- Creating small world scenes

- Orienteering using a compass or the sun

- Creating sun dials to track time

- Wild flower hunt

- Pond dipping

- Placing and arranging

- Sticky wellies (use a strip of double sided tape and stick it to children's welly boots)

- Tree faces (made with mud or clay)

- Constructing fairy/elf houses

- Den building

- Animal habitats – make a bird boxes, hedgehog home or stag beetle stumpery

- Building bug houses – using sticks, leaves, grass and other resources

- Shadow puppets – suspend a white sheet in a suitable place and make shadow puppets with hands or using natural resources

- Memory games, Pass the pine cone – children sit in a circle and pass around a pine cone. A person sitting in the middle of the circle (closes his eyes) and after a period of time he/she says 'stop!'. Whoever is holding the cone becomes the person in the middle.

- Create and use representation for communication (such as creating mud painting and pies)

- Make music and respond to rhythm by using natural objects

- Construct small world models outdoors.

Practical activities for children under three

There are many activities practitioners can introduce with children under three. Many of the activities for children over three can be adapted to this age range. However, here are some tried and tested favourites seen in practice.

- Forest School soup – putting a variety of objects in a bowl and stirring it into a natural concoction

- Feely bag or mat – objects are placed on a mat or in a bag for children to reach for and handle

- Forest School hats – double-sided tape is attached to card and children can stick on leaves and other natural objects to make a hat or a crown

- Mark making with mud and natural dyes – mixing up mud or squishing berries in yogurt pots and using a variety of natural objects to make marks or prints

- Sticky wellies – attaching double-sided tape on wellies and sticking on objects found while outdoors

- Where is Squirrel? – hiding soft toy (ideally one representing British wildlife) in various locations and asking the children to identify where it is using positional language

- Natural shakers or instruments – put objects in a yogurt pot, cover the open end with paper and an elastic band to make a shaker

- Voice play – mimicking sounds heard in nature or sounds created by each other

- Stories/poems – using props, puppets, to support stories, poems, songs and rhymes from a selection of cultures

- Reflection – using shatter proof mirrors to objects and reflections. You will need to ensure that children do not aim mirrors at the sun

- Collecting – baskets, paper shopping bags, boxes, buckets, can be used to collect natural objects. These can be looked and discussed as a group

- Mark making – using paint brushes to make marks on trees and other objects with mud and water.

Planning for the season

Planning for Forest School starts with observation. Observation may initially take place at nursery, if the children have not been out before. The observer will need to look, listen and note what sparks children's curiosity and fosters deep involvement indoors and outdoors. Reflecting upon, assessing and analysing observations will tell practitioners the types of experiences and opportunities they should plan for during Forest School.

Good practice involves consulting children and parents on what has been observed, rather than making assumptions,

Developing a Forest School in Early Years Provision

particularly as children's thinking is often divergent from our own. Children need to be consulted about their learning environments and adults working with children should be involving children in planning and evaluating Forest School sessions.

By tuning-in to children's lines of inquiry, practitioners can plan sessions which are meaningful and exciting. Particular seasons will lend themselves particularly well to learning about certain themes or topics.

Seasonal changes will redecorate your Forest School site; allowing for exciting learning opportunities. Cyclical changes are important in nature and giving children first-hand experiences and observation of these will help develop their understanding and appreciation of the world around them. Knowing what to expect during each season will support practitioners in planning activities which will interest children and extend their understanding of what they experience through the environment around them.

Below are seasons and experiences you may consider incorporating into your planning but it is important to remember that activities should be based as far as possible on children's interests and suggestions.

Autumn

During the autumn animals are busy preparing for the winter months ahead. They will be busy eating to add extra fat or preparing food stores for the winter months.

Berries ranging in shape, size and colour will be found on plants like ivy, brambles and trees such as elder and hawthorn, holly, rowan. Animals such as squirrels will be busy collecting, eating and burying nuts.

During this time trees produce a range of seeds, for example:

- Sycamore, ash and field maple produce large winged seed.

- Alder, larch, cedar and pine produce cones.

- Silver birch produce catkins.

- Oak, horse chestnut and sweet chestnut produce nuts.

Children will enjoy discovering, investigating and collecting these objects.

Autumn is a good time to explore seed dispersal and examine how some of the seeds are designed to be carried in the wind, dispersed in water or eaten and dispersed by wildlife.

There will be a wide range of resources on the ground for children to collect and use in play.

Damp and darker conditions arising in late autumn bring rise to an array of fungi such as mushrooms and lichen. Children may be able to spot where fungi have been nibbled by animals such as squirrels. In the interest of health and safety, young children should not be encourages to touch fungi or lichen.

Spiderwebs will become more noticeable to young eyes as they glisten in morning dew; however, as the season becomes increasingly cooler, insects will take shelter or become less active or die.

Autumn things to do:

- Printing using natural objects and paint, mud or clay.

- Organising scavenger hunts for autumn treasures.

- Making leaf crowns.

- Matching or sorting collections by varying criteria.

- Collecting, identifying and organising specimens such as leaves (by colour and shape), fruits or seeds.

- Placing and arranging natural objects.

- Seeing how many patterns can be created by putting leaves in different positions such as repetition, alternation, rotation and reflection.

- Building a leaf pit for children to throw, jump in, kick, walk and run through.

- Creating a photographic reference of plants with protective devices such as thorns, stings, spikes, spurs, thick cuticle, and poison.

- Make observations of migratory birds such as geese, swallows and swifts.

- Collecting, counting or hiding conkers or acorns.

Children should not be encouraged to touch fungi unless you are absolutely sure it is safe. Children should not be encouraged to play with yew and ivy berries as they are poisonous if ingested.

Adults can get children thinking about and involved with the preparation of warm drinks and food and the effects these have on our bodies on cold days. Cold days are also an ideal time for children to feel the effects activity and exercise has on the body. When appropriate, campfires can be introduced as resource which humans use to produce heat for warmth and cooking.

Being outside during the winter will foster meaningful opportunities to develop children's thinking and understanding of how animals and insects have found ways to adapt and survive by keeping warm, conserving energy, hibernating or migrating during winter months.

Many trees will be stripped bare, providing opportunities to discuss what this means for animals and insects that take shelter in trees or feed off them.

Spotting bird's nests and squirrel's dreys will be much easier when trees have lost their foliage and with the support of adults, children can learn how to distinguish between the two. The children may witness squirrels clambering up trees with mouthfuls of leaves for their drey. This is an ideal time to discuss which insects and animals can still be seen and which have disappeared from view.

Adults can challenge children to find ways to identify trees and shrubs through their bark, branches and buds and by looking at the leaves on the ground near the plant. These plants may also produce flowers, fruits and seeds which will be of interest to the children.

Winter is a great time for adults to extend children's vocabulary and understanding of deciduous and coniferous trees and shrubs.

Through practical activities in the natural environment, children can investigate how deciduous trees lose foliage at the end of the typical growing season while coniferous, trees and shrubs such as pines, spruces, firs, cedars, and junipers evergreens keep their foliage. Some of the twigs and branches from these plants can be used in activities

- Using your imagination to create a home for a fairy or elf.

- Design clothing or dwellings for flower fairies, using books and illustrations of Cicely Mary Barker as inspiration.

- Finding fungi such as mushrooms that have been nibbled.

- Creating your own webs and weaves, using string and incorporating grasses and other natural resources.

- Making forest mud pies, stews and potions and recording the recipes.

Winter

Winter offers many unique and meaningful experiences and is an ideal time to take children outdoors.

The cooler weather encourages children to think about how to dress appropriately and stay active to keep warm. Children will develop their understanding of dressing appropriately through checking the weather and discussing as a group how keep warm.

such as weaving, shelter building and for bending into weaves, or wands.

Winter things to do:

- Discovering winter colours in nature using paint swatches or palates created with natural resources.

- Bird watching and identification.

- Looking after birds by making bird feeders.

- Collecting and organising specimens such as twigs from deciduous trees or leaves from evergreens.

- Creating shelters or dens for animals.

- Building towers or shelters with sticks.

- Identifying winter havens for insects – log piles, heaps of leaves, inside seed casings or cracks and crevices on buildings.

- Making bug homes or hotels.

- Freezing natural objects in ice and watching them thaw.

- Looking at patterns made from frost or ice.

- Observing and identifying our own and animal tracks in snow or mud.

- Making snowmen and snow angels.

- Creating tree faces out of clay and natural resources.

- Listening to and recording winter sounds.

- Using digital photography to document winter.

- Creating a campfire to keep warm.

- Preparing a warm drink using a Kelly Kettle or pouring drinks from a thermos or flask.

Spring

Spring is a major time for growth and change. Insects and animals will become more active. Keep your eyes open for flying and ground-based insects. This is an ideal time for children to explore life cycles of insects and animals. The life cycles of insects such as the ladybird or butterfly and animals such as frogs, toads and newts are most readily observed during this period so look out for resources to help with the identification of stages.

Each month, there will be new buds, shoots and flowers to see, starting with snowdrops, crocuses and early tree blossom. There will be a wide range of colours on display.

Many birds choose to make their nests in spring in preparation for laying and bring up chicks. Children can explore the design of nests and investigate how they are able to stay together, withstand weather and hold the weight of birds and eggs through making their own models.

Children can also listen out for bird calls and songs used to attract mates. There will be plenty of sounds from birds, rustling feet, squirrels racing up and along trees and insects on the move. The sounds of grasses and leaves blowing in the wind or the pitter pattering of raindrops will also capture the attention of young children.

CASE STUDY: TREES

In one setting I visited, practitioners had used children's interests in trees to develop their learning about them in a very personal and meaningful way. Each child had chosen a favourite tree on their Forest School site. They explained to the adults what they liked about their tree. The children's answers varied widely and it was interesting to read their comments. Some children liked how tall or wide their tree was, while others liked its shape, making comparisons to animals or imaginary creatures (such as monsters). There were also children who liked their tree because of its foliage, flowers or seeds (such as conkers) or because it had interesting bark or holes.

Throughout the year, the children documented changes to their trees and kept a record of aspects which interested them. The children were actively involved in collecting tree artefacts, making bark rubbings, recording seasonal changes through digital photography, producing drawings or paintings and observing and recording wildlife which took an interest in their tree.

Spring showers will provide ample opportunities for designing water proof shelters, splashing in puddles and collecting rain water for making imaginary potions and stews.

Spring things to do:

- Conducting minibeast hunts.

- Hunting for insects or animals but being aware not to disturb them.

- Collecting and organising photos or specimens of natural objects such as plants with interesting smells. Collections can also be made by gathering and pressing wildflowers of the month; tree flowers that come before leaves in the (early spring) and those that come after leaves (late spring).

- Making birds nest on a small or large scale (for children to climb inside).

- Planning texture hunts by looking for things that are tickly, soft, hard, bumpy, spikey, prickly, smooth, silky, rough and brittle.

- Going on sound walks using recordable devices.

- Creating music makers created using natural objects.

- Creating your own spring sound scape by combining the sounds of your music makers and instruments in the setting.

- Building a waterproof shelter.

- Developing a potion or perfume by crushing petals and other things collected from the floor.

- Using paint swatches to compare to colours in the natural environment.

- Develop your own palate of spring colours using paint or samples of colour found in the environment.

Summer

During the summer animals and insects are most active. Children may come across newts, frogs and toads, or

TOP TIP

When collecting natural objects, try to only collect objects from the forest floor. Unnecessary collection and destruction of plants must be avoided. It is important to inform children of any rarities in the natural environment which should not be touched, picked or trampled upon. Remind children not to put anything they find near or in their mouth and to wash their hands after play.

Summer things to do:

- Making models with clay and natural resources.

- Collecting and organising photos or specimens of natural objects such as leaves, flowers and roots.

- Children can examine things that damage and alter plants such as fungi, leaf feeders and galls.

- Scent trails – children can also be encouraged to look for things that smell and use vocabulary to describe scents.

- Planning a treasure hunt, designing maps and trail markers.

- Making mud pies and Forest School potions and stews.

- Creating shadow puppets using your hands or creating a shadow guessing game using objects found outdoors.

- Going on blindfold walks in pairs.

- Listening to and recording sounds.

- Designing your own set of wings inspired by a pollinating insect or a bird.

pollinating insects or feathers from moulting birds. In areas where there are ponds or lakes, children may get to see nature water fowl with young.

There will be plenty of colours to see, sounds to hear and scents to smell. There may even be opportunities to taste nature through activities such as making berry jams, cordials or crumbles.

The sun will be at its strongest; making it an ideal time to observe the effects of heat on the body and discussing ways to keep ourselves safe in the heat. The warm weather allows for meaningful discussion of appropriate clothing such as the use of hats, light, long-sleeved shirts and trousers or leggings to protect skin from the sun, stings, bites and scratches. The importance of appropriate footwear will be emphasised through children's desires to climb trees or navigate varied terrain. Children will enjoy taking part in creating dens or shelters for shade and preparing cool drinks and picnics.

Once children are able to recognise the effects the sun has on them, they will be ready to explore the effects it has on nature. With the support of adults, they can begin to identify ways plants, animals and insects keep cool and maintain hydration.

As described in Chapter 3, it is necessary to build in sufficient time for reflection, for consulting children about spontaneous and planned experiences that take place at different times of year. Different settings have used various ways to capture the voice of the child. Mind maps, recordable devices, children's drawings, video, photography and objects collected sessions are powerful ways children can communicate their experiences. Using a Forest School puppet or soft toy to communicate with children may help them feel more at ease when reflecting. Showing a snippet of video captured during a session may also be effective at getting children to talk. Exploring past events or, problems encountered, providing feedback to peers, contemplating ideas, questions through group discussion offer children opportunities to think critically. Children may need help realising that adults are learners as well and that adults may have developed misconceptions too. Practitioners will need to experiment with a range of methods to discover which ones are most effective for individual learners. Adults can model being an effective learner for children by:

- Sharing with children their thinking

- Asking questions and finding out answers

- Being reflective

- Sharing what they have learnt and how.

Children's photos act as a prompt to remind them and their peers what happened during a session and over a series of sessions.

Photographs can also provide power insight into their thoughts, feelings and perspectives of the world around them.

EXTENDED LEARNING FROM TREES

Forest School practitioners in one setting used children's interest in trees to extend their learning through planned activities, during the summer term.

A balance of adult-led and child-led activities included:

- Making elder pencils and elder cordial

- Matching and identifying a set of leaves to trees using ID sheets

- Sorting or classifying leaves

- Designing wood cookies also known as wood discs or medallions

- Reading stories such as *The Lonely Tree* by Nick Halliday or *Stickman* by Julia Donaldson or *Stanley's Stick* by Neal Layton. (See **Further resources**.)

- Making story or journey sticks

- Climbing trees

- Looking at tree houses and dens

- Measuring height and determining the age of trees

- Making clay faces/tree spirits

- Painting and printing with objects from trees

- Examining products made from trees (wood) in the home and school environment

- Exploring the importance of trees to humans, animals and insects.

TOP TIP

Children can learn to conserve, value and respect nature through good role models. Children who are tempted to pick flowers, berries, drop rubbish, break branches off trees and shrubs will need someone to explain the importance of respecting nature and how Forest School is home to an array of wildlife.

Inviting the children to talk about their photos by saying things like: 'Tell me about this photo…' is a great way of entering the child's world. Children should be encouraged to paste what they view as significant photographs into their documentation books or incorporate them into a display. Staff can help the children annotate them or display them on boards or in digital formats.

Representations from their experiences will help convey to other children and adults how and what they are learning at Forest School and make connections between experiences.

Tools

Although tools are not an essential part of good Forest School sessions, they can add a valuable extra element to developing the learner's confidence and give the opportunity to achieve and create something special. Often tools are not used with groups because the practitioner is not confident themselves. So much is covered on the leader training and tools are just one part of a very comprehensive programme, but there are many CPD courses that focus on tools. It is worth contacting an approved Forest School training provider to see what is on offer.

We have seen tools introduced in a variety of ways to young children. In one setting, the entire group worked on tool use together. The Forest School leader demonstrated how to use the tool and then the children were encouraged to have a go. The problem with this is that not all of the children will want to do it, some may not be interested or see the relevance and others will want more time to observe. Children are very capable of telling adults when they are ready to try something or when they want more time to watch or practice skills.

In Denmark we saw excellent modelling of tool use by adults. Adults modelled tool use in everyday activities with the children. The children would observe as the adult explained what he or she was doing. When the child was ready, they would ask the adult for a go. This is how the adults knew the children were interested and ready to learn how to use the tool. There was also a central place were tools were kept and could be signed out by users. Here, the children would see an adult to self-select and sign out tools they wanted to use in for a particular purpose. Children would discuss with the adult what they wanted to do and adults would offer support in the tool selection and by demonstrating how to use it. By having this system in place, children felt ownership over the process while adults could carefully monitor children using tools.

Tools used by Forest Schools include: bow saws, penknives, billhooks, loppers, secateurs and hand drills. The main tools used with early year's children are vegetable peelers, penknives, bow saws and hand drills. Before using tools with a group it is important to consider your own practice. Are you able to correctly model how to use the tool? Have you carried out the necessary risk assessment on the tool being used? Practitioners will need to model good practice to ensure safe use and to encourage children to think about safety points and the consequences of improper use. Most settings adopt a 1:1 adult support when children are using tools. The adults keep track of the tools by having clear systems in place such as counting equipment 'out' (in the beginning) and 'in' (at the end) during the session or by having signing 'out' and 'in' sheets.

When using tools with young children, it is important to consider the following:

- Is the purpose for using the tool relevant? Is the learner or group of learners ready for tool use? (For example, have they demonstrated an ability to listen and follow instructions?).

Penknives are often a progression from using a vegetable peeler. Children can practice the action needed to use a knife by peeling carrots or other vegetables for snack or soup making. However, peelers are not appropriate for whittling and are not the safer option as bark will often get lodged in the blade and need to be cleared which can result in cuts. Practitioners should not be teaching children to use tools inappropriately or encourage the use of tools which are not fit for purpose.

Penknives are often introduced to scrape bark from a stick to act as a toasting utensil, which in time will lead to whittling. Whittling is a very calming and satisfying experience for many. (Leaders wishing to find out more may be interested in 'Knife Use with Groups, Forest School Leader's Guide' written by Liz Knowles in consultation with the Forest School Training Network and available from www.muddyfaces.co.uk.) Bow saws may be introduced when there is a need for sawing wood for a fire or making wood cookies. Again, it is important the tool is fit for purpose (for example, it has the correct blade for the wood needing to be sawn and is in good condition). These points are covered during Forest School training. Bow saws are useful for fostering co-operation and developing shoulder muscles, which in turn aids emergent writing skills. Hand drills are required for making holes. It is useful to have a range of bit sizes suitable for use with wood. Again, make sure the drill and bits are in good condition and the learner is working on a stable surface.

Forest School leaders should keep an inventory of tools ensuring that they are stored correctly and safely. Tools will require cleaning after use and regular maintenance. When not in use, tools should be kept in a locked unit.

Good quality tools are expensive and it is a good idea to wait until you feel the group or particular learners are ready to use tools before embarking on purchasing equipment. Often just one of each tool is required plus safety gloves, storage and maintenance equipment is needed to start off with. Some local authorities offer a lending service where tools can be borrowed for a period of time. This is very useful when you are just starting out and budgets are at a premium.

Open-ended resources found in nature

There is a world out there beyond these walls that is waiting to be discovered…the most well-resourced classroom! There is no need for expensive man-made toys when you have natural resources!

The nursery garden can provide rich outdoor experiences but there are far more open-ended resources in the natural world and these offer new challenge, excitement and learning opportunities. The flexibility and adaptable characteristics of natural objects make them ideal resources to promote creativity. Close encounters to experience nature will help them learn about the world around them.

Adults must carry out thorough risk assessments to gauge risk and hazards. Learn about the wildlife in your area. Some plants are poisonous if ingested. Children should not be encouraged to handle items that may seriously harm them or cause irritation. Clear boundaries must be in place to ensure that children do not put anything in their mouth while at Forest School and to wash their hands after handling natural objects. However, this does not mean sterilising everything and eliminating all forms of dirt. Research shows that children who are exposed to healthy bacteria, parasites, and viruses will develop a much stronger immune system.

Natural resources children enjoy exploring include:

- Logs and stumps

- Sticks

- Pine cones

- Snail shells

- Feathers

- Rocks, stones of varying sizes and textures

- Wood, green and dead, rotting wood, wood chipping.

- Soil

- Water

- Natural hideaways

- Mud

- Grass

- Seeds, pods and fruits from plants

- Moss

- Green and flowering plants

- Leaf litter

- Fungi and lichen (although, children should not be encouraged to touched these unless they are assessed as being absolutely safe).

Mud kitchens

Allowing children to play with mud not only allows them to explore the world around them, relax and have fun, but (as mentioned previously) exposes them to healthy bacteria which strengthens their immune system.

The National Wildlife Federation (based in the United States of America) has produced a report: 'The Dirt on Dirt' which reveals how getting dirty can be healthy and fun. The full report can be downloaded from: http://www.nwf.org/get-outside/be-out-there/why-be-out-there/benefits/the-dirt-on-dirt.aspx

Designing a mud kitchen is a great way of promoting messy and creative forms of play. It is also a great way to celebrate 'International Mud Day'. International Mud Day is organised by the World Forum Foundation which brings together children and early childhood professionals from around the world.

TOP TIP

Before using tools ensure you have:

- Assessed through observation, the appropriateness of introducing tools – Are the children ready? What is the purpose?

- Confidence in your skills and ability to model correct tool use with children

- Included policy and procedures for tool use in your handbook

- Completed risk assessments

- Emergency procedures are in place, in the rare event of an accident.

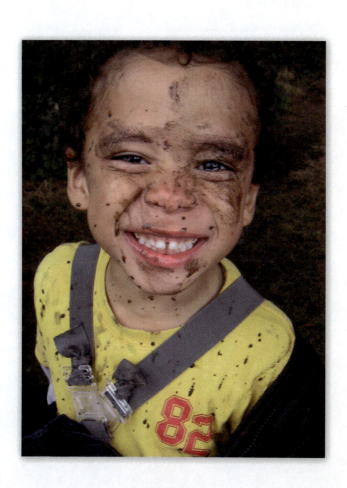

For ideas on mud kitchens, do an Internet-based image search for 'mud kitchens' or visit 'Making a Mud Kitchen' at http://www.muddyfaces.co.uk/mudkitchen.php

Storytelling at Forest School

There are many wonderful ways of stories being told or acted out at Forest School.

Here are some examples:

- Story sticks – attaching natural resources to a stick using string, tape and pipe cleaners (the items attached are significant to the story).

- Planting props – adults plant a prop for the children to find outdoors (such as a mitten or tiny tea set) and the group creates a story about whose it is and how it got there.

- Group story – one person starts off the story and each person weaves in their ideas by adding descriptive words or a sentence.

- Oral storytelling – retelling familiar stories and/or adding your own twists to characters or a storyline. In one setting a practitioner had adapted a story about three little pigs to be three little hedgehogs and linked the story with a practical activity involving building dens. Familiar storylines can be adapted include animals, people and situations experienced at Forest School.

- Using puppets to tell stories – puppets can be ones made from nature or from the setting.

- Incorporating shadows – shadow puppet made from hands or natural objects.

- Using props – giving all children natural props to bring up at different points in the story to add to the storyline.

- Producing actions or words – giving children a sequence of actions or words to be used at various stages in a story.

- Painting faces – to support acting out parts of a story or for role play.

TOP TIP

Find ways to:

- Link stories with elements from the Forest School environment and with spontaneous and planned activities

- Involve children, staff and families in the storytelling process

- Share stories from other cultures.

- Incorporating sound effects – a storyteller in one setting I visited used an owl whistle when reading *Owl Babies* by Martin Waddlell (Waddell, M.(2006) *Owl Babies*, Walker, London).

- Role play – painting faces or making masks to support children and staff acting as characters in stories

- Substitution – substituting the names of characters for the names of children and staff.

- Using scents, sounds and textures found in the environment to contribute to storytelling.

Chapter 5: Involving colleagues and parents

Effective communication plays an important part in the creation of successful partnerships with colleagues and with parents. Getting it right will determine how effective settings will be at getting other colleagues parents or professionals involved with Forest School.

When communicating with colleagues and parents, there are a number of considerations.

Firstly, practitioners must consider the characteristics of the audience being addressed. When communicating with adults, consider the purpose and method of communication. Establish if the purpose of communication is to: gather information, consult, discuss, seek collaboration, make request, inform, persuade, or motivate.

Allowing for time to find out about the audience in advance will help practitioners plan what to say and how to deliver the information. Have a clear indication of your audience's level of knowledge, skills and understanding surrounding Forest Schools and outdoor practice. This may involve conducting informal consultations, such as chatting with colleagues or parents before or after school or thorough more formal methods such as questionnaires.

Parent advisory group meetings or governor's meetings can be a great springboard for introducing ideas and gathering initial feedback.

Establish parent reps who you know will support what you are trying to do and will help keep other parents informed. Parent reps can help convey messages to other parents both through face-to-face contact and via email. Parent reps can also be instrumental in finding volunteers and organising fundraising events for buying Forest School kit and equipment.

Letters, posters, leaflets and websites will help you communicate with some of your audience, but most settings with Forest School programmes will maintain that face-to-face communication is most effective. This can be achieved through open sessions, workshops and information sessions.

If introducing colleagues to the idea of starting a Forest School programme, consider what they need to know. They may need a brief explanation of what Forest Schools is, where it originated, relevant research, pedagogy and practice. In addition, it could include examples of local schools which have started successful programmes and links to Early Years Foundation Stage developmental matters, policy (school policies or government) and reports (such as Ofsted).

Audience response

As communication is a two-way process, be sure to factor in time for the audience to respond to what you are communicating. Encourage them to ask questions, share their views and concerns. Putting together an agenda for the audience will show them the structure of the session or workshop and inform them on what will be covered. When

addressing adults, it is important to consider their diverse learning needs. Copies of notes and presentation slides and post-session minutes will help foster further reflection and remind participants of important information and points raised.

An one hour introductory meeting with colleagues may be structured as follows:

- 15 minutes of information

- 10 minutes answering questions

- 15 minutes discussion involving sharing views and addressing reservations

- 15 minutes of motivating through a practical outdoor activity

- Five minutes on working towards a decision or planning next steps.

A nice way to introduce Forest School to colleagues or parents is to get the adults to think of memorable outdoor play experiences they had as a child. This can then be followed by a slide show of photographs or through a short video clip. If possible, use photographs or a short video clip from the setting; however, if these are not available, there are several video clips on Forest School which can be viewed online. (You can find these by doing an Internet-based search of 'Forest School Video Clip'.) Be sure to ask the audience thought-provoking questions afterwards.

Such questions may include:

- What were your thoughts as you watched that video?

- How did the footage make you feel?

- Do you feel children today are getting enough of these sorts of experiences in school or at home? Do you feel these experiences are important to children why or why not?

You may then want to ask your audience to think about the setting's outdoor environment.

- What opportunities are there for children to access nature?

- Are the grounds inspiring? The outdoor environment should be inspiring to the children and adults. Outdoor environments that lack nature and are too static become boring for children and adults alike. Exciting outdoor environments can foster creative play and improve children's access to positive adult interaction.

- What is missing? Are there open-ended natural resources available such as: leaves, puddles, logs, sticks, rocks, puddles, mud, scrubs for natural hideaways?

- Is there the potential to increase the biodiversity? Can you create a wild space, plant willow or trees, ash log piles, scrubs and grass?

Questions

Remember that colleagues and parents will have questions for you too. It is useful to consider in advance the questions they may ask so you can prepare your answers. If you get stuck, ask a colleague, friend or a parent to tell you what they would want to know. You may need to do some background reading and investigative works, to ensure you are prepared for questions. There are several books and journal articles available describing different Forest School programmes in a range of settings (see page 91). You may also want to consider contacting settings with established programmes and asking them how they addressed questions from colleagues and parents.

Parents and colleagues are likely to want to know the answers to the following:

- Where will Forest School take place?

- How will the children get to the site?

- What is the ratio of adults to children?

- How will the children be kept safe along busy roads or once on site?

- How long will the children be out for?

- What will the children do?

- Will the children have a drink or snack?

- What will happen if a child or adult needs the toilet?

- What is the role of the Forest School leader and other adults?

- What happens if someone gets hurt or becomes ill or needs to go back while the group are out?

- What if a child has allergies?

- What if child doesn't have appropriate clothes for going out?

- What happens if a child needs a spare change of clothes while out?

- How will we prevent children from getting lost?

- Will there be parents or volunteers to help us?

Rather than simply answering all the questions yourself and risk appearing as the only expert in the room, open the question up for other adults in the room to answer. Ask your audience to contribute to answers to open-ended questions, for example: "What are your suggestions on how we could address this?". This will ensure the meeting remains interactive and two-way. It is important that the group leaves the meeting feeling that they have been involved and consulted, as this will create a sense of ownership in the planning process.

After hearing what others have suggested, you can give your response. You may find that they have answered their own question or have come up with solutions you never considered. Be prepared to give the reasoning for your answers. For example, if you say that there should be a 1:4 ratio; be sure to explain that your reasoning stems from information obtained from school policies for outings, books, websites, other settings, research or Forest School training companies. You will probably also need to ask the group how they think you could achieve such as a high ratio. You can then give them examples of how other settings have dealt with this.

Making assumptions

Communication can fail for many reasons. However it is most likely to fail because an inaccurate assumption has been made by either the person delivering the information or the person receiving it.

Be sensitive to how your message may be received. Acknowledge what colleagues and parent are already doing. Admit to colleagues or parents when you do not feel you

have a complete picture, let them know when you feel may have formed a misconception that needs clarifying. This may also prevent the offended colleague or parent from assuming that the setting thinks they might be getting it wrong.

Building confidence through progression

When developing a Forest School, it is necessary to not only look at where the child is at, but where the practitioners are at, where the families are at and indeed where the setting is at. The needs and interests of individuals as well as the group must be considered. Forest School leaders may need to think about offering progressions for adults and children, such as building up the amount of time spent at a Forest School site from an hour up to a full day. Progressions may also apply to the amount of space the children have access to. Some Forest Schools section off an area of natural space or forest with boundary tape and over time the area is broadened to include additional areas the children want to explore.

Practitioners will need to be sensitive to the needs and insecurities of children, parents and colleagues, as some will be less comfortable in outdoor environments. The length of time it takes for a colleague to become comfortable in taking children out in natural spaces will depend on the breadth of their personal and professional experience and their exposure to a variety of outdoor environments. The amount of training and support they have received will influence the quality of outdoor play and learning experiences they are able to facilitate in a range of contexts and environments.

The length of time it takes a child to become comfortable and independent at Forest School will depend on factors such as age, stage in development, needs and exposure to environments outside of their educational setting and home.

Practitioners need to be able to recognise when it is appropriate to push children and adults beyond their comfort zone to broaden their experiences and further their development.

It can often be that the children and adults who express a dread of going out, need and benefit from it the most.

It is important to remember that everyone has something they are good at and enjoy doing. By tapping into the interests, cultural backgrounds, skills and knowledge of children, colleagues, and parents, Forest School practitioners

- Hosting weekend taster events for working parents and families from the local community.

- Providing feedback through questionnaires and evaluations of events or programmes.

Practitioners must consider barriers to parental involvement. Discuss with colleagues ways you can support parental participation from those whose first language is not English, those who are working full-time, fathers and families with younger or older siblings. Your Parent Advisory Group is likely to be able to offer you many useful suggestions to support parents in becoming involved.

Collaborating and networking with other professionals Planning visits to other settings can help practitioners gain an understanding of the range of practice, considerations and adaptations which have been made to cater to the needs of individual settings.

While on visits, it is important to ask questions, and seek clarification on the visits. Reflect on what you observe and share your thoughts with the professionals you are with. Comment on what you like but be confident to question or seek clarification on an aspect of their practice you do not understand or agree with. Rather than walking away with a misconception or inaccurate assumption, seek clarification from the professionals in non-critical and confrontational manner. Remember that

can find ways to incorporate these so everyone feels able to participate and make a valued contribution to the sessions.

Involving and collaborating with parents

Parents can get involved in a variety of ways.

Practitioners can encourage parental involvement by:

- Inviting them to join sessions – this could be done through the key person and the child.

- Planning open days for them to attend with their children.

- Organising 'Parents and Parks' days – a time when families, children and staff can enjoy playing and joining in activities in a local park and sharing a picnic.

- Encouraging parents to share in documenting their child's comments and learning from sessions. This may also involve inviting them to come in to print off photos and pasting them in children's documentation profiles.

TOP TIP

In areas where Forest School practice is well established, there may be support networks for practitioners. These networks may provide e-newsletters and meetings or training. They may also be able to link practitioners to:

- Funding bodies

- Forest School mentors

- Equipment borrowing schemes

- Volunteers

- Supporting organisations

- Minibus hire.

a setting may have valid reasons for organising sessions or conducting practice in a particular way and you may need to seek clarification to develop a complete picture.

To find Forest Schools in your area, conduct web-based searches and ask advisors at your local authority if they know of local settings you can link up with. Visits can be arranged by phone, email or by writing to the setting. Educational settings tend to be very busy places so try not to get discouraged if your first attempts to make contact are not successful. You may need to experiment using a range of methods of communication before you get a reply.

Some settings will allow you to visit for free while others may charge a small fee. Fees are generally charged as a means to fundraise or support sustainability and further development of the Forest School programme. Collaborating with other professionals involves supporting each other by sharing good practice, exposing challenges and barriers and coming up with solutions. It should be a two-way process of sharing. Your setting may be able to negotiate the fee to be waived in return for offering to share good practice taking place in your setting or offering a reciprocal visit.

Groups

You may discover through your contacts that there is a local Forest School Cluster or Network Group operating in your area. If there isn't already a network in your area, invite other professionals to help you form one.

Organisations such as the Institute for Outdoor Learning (IOL) have a Forest School Special Interest Group. Through the group, members can find of local training events and network with professionals who share similar interests and passions.

Childminders and settings offering Forest School can find ways of teaming up with each other by contacting local authority advisors or childminding networks. Childminders can be invited on sessions and to network meetings.

Collaborating with a range of early years professionals from the community can be a mutually rewarding collaboration, fostering an atmosphere of learning from and supporting each other. It also gives children the opportunity to develop relationships, play and learn alongside children and adults from the wider community.

CASE STUDY: NETWORKING

Eastwood's group was established in 2008 following a local Forest School Training course. Professionals on the course wanted to stay in contact, support and share practice. Current members include Forest School professionals from other schools, college and university lecturers and students, FE students, early years advisors, head teachers, early years managers, representatives from parks and the community. The school has also built a website and created a social networking site to network and collaborate with other professionals.

Eastwood Nursery School's Forest School and Outdoor Play Network Group

Successful collaboration of professionals through networks or cluster groups happens when:

- Professionals (from a variety of professional backgrounds) are open to different ways of working

- An atmosphere of sharing a range of skills and expertise is encouraged

- An appropriate and convenient space is identified for the group to meet on a regular basis.

When working with parents, colleagues or other professionals, it is important to be reflective and sensitive to their training, backgrounds, experiences, needs and interests. Forest School provisions will differ from setting to setting; they will be as unique as the staff, children and families who create them. It is important to consider that what may work in one setting, may not work in another.

Chapter 6: Growth of Forest School in the UK

Since Forest School was bought to the UK from Denmark in 1993 by Bridgwater College, Forest School has grown from strength to strength. It is probably the fastest growing movement in education that has come from the grass roots; the practitioners and not been imposed by government.

As more trainers have come on board, it is almost impossible to know actually how many practitioners have trained to be Forest School leaders, but it is estimated to be approximately 9,000 in 2012. How many of these are regularly running Forest School, again is an unknown quantity. Also the number of practitioners who have trained does not necessarily reflect the numbers who have qualified. One of the arguments for developing a National Governing Body is to have a central database of trained personnel.

Local authorities

Several local authorities and statutory bodies in the UK have embraced Forest School – especially for early years children. Worcestershire and Oxfordshire county councils were two of the first authorities to invite Bridgwater College to offer outreach Level 3 leader training to practitioners. Both authorities subsequently appointed coordinators to develop Forest School in their county.

Twelve years on and Forest School in these counties continues to grow. So why have these authorities, during times of austerity, continued to support this initiative? Mainly this is because officers at a strategic level believe in the value of outdoor learning and in particular, acknowledge

CASE STUDY: WORCESTERSHIRE COUNTY COUNCIL

In 1999, senior officers from Worcestershire visited Bridgwater College and accompanied a group of children from the early excellence centre to Forest School. They were inspired by everything they saw and heard during their visit and agreed they wanted to offer this experience to Worcestershire children. In 2000 a partnership between the Early Years and Childcare Partnership, the Education Directorate and Bishops Wood Environmental Centre found the monies to appoint a coordinator for 12 months. The project was to run across the maintained, voluntary and private sectors.

A Forest School site was developed at Bishops Wood Centre and three settings were invited to participate; an inner city maintained nursery with a high proportion of children with English as an additional language, a private nursery from a rural area that frequently used local woodland and a voluntary playgroup that had no outdoor area. Children were collected by minibus and taken to Bishops Wood Centre. The children attended for one session per week from October through to the following July.

During the year other settings asked to join the project including one school who asked to come on board because the daughter of the head teacher attended with one of the pilot groups. Even though this family spent a lot of time outdoors already, he could see how Forest School had impacted on the self-confidence of his daughter and wanted to give the children in his reception class the same opportunity.

At the end of the year, outcomes for children were evaluated in several ways. Firstly, staff from the setting had been given three questionnaires. One at the beginning of the programme (a simple base line assessment), one halfway through and one at the end of the programme, asking about progress shown for individual children, the group as a whole and any changes in staff attitudes.

All the evaluations showed the children had made very good progress. This cannot be put down solely to Forest School as most of the evidence was anecdotal. However, the staff reported the children who had attended Forest School made significant progress in PSED and children with English as an additional language were talking more freely when out in the woodland. The private setting reported how the group had bonded and supported each other in transition into school.

An interesting outcome was that dads came to Forest School on a regular basis which had a really positive effect on the groups. The dads reported they felt out of place in the nursery, on the whole a female-dominated environment, but they felt relaxed and comfortable in the woods. It wasn't the fact we sometimes had fires or used tools, they really felt the children, especially the boys, were learning more and were more purposeful and motivated at Forest School.

Staff also reported positive outcomes in their practice. They felt they had more opportunity to stand back and observe the children in a different environment. They realised the value simple open-ended equipment afforded the children. They were surprised by the creativity shown, the thinking skills and problem solving observed but most of all the richness of the deep-level learning that was happening.

Involvement scale

Secondly, a small-scale research project was also used as an evaluation tool. A practitioner undertaking professional development came to Forest School. She followed one group over a period of seven months both at Forest School and in their setting, using Ferre Laevers levels (Laevers 1994) of involvement scale as an observation tool. This showed that children were regularly operating at levels 4 and 5 at Forest School and lower levels in the setting.

Level 4 is described as 'continuous activity with intense moments'. The child's activity has intense moments during which activities at level 3 can come to have special meaning. Level 4 is reserved for the kind of activity seen in those intense moments, and can be deducted from the 'involvement signals'. This level of activity is resumed after interruptions. Stimuli, from the surrounding environment, however attractive, cannot seduce the child away from the activity. Level 5 is operating at 'sustained intense activity'. The child shows continuous and intense activity revealing the greatest involvement. In the observed period, not all the signals for involvement need to be there, but the essential ones must be present: concentration, creativity, energy and persistence. The intensity must be present for almost all the observation period.

Observing areas of learning was also a surprise. Out of the six areas of learning, Communication, Language and Literacy came out on top. Children had so many opportunities to talk peer to peer, child to adult, in small and large groups.

Parents/carers were also involved in the evaluation and reported how they were surprised at the cross fertilisation of skills. One parent wrote, "at the weekend my husband decided to prune our conifers. Jamie asked what he was going to do with the bow saw. When he was told Jamie said: "we use that at Forest School. You need a glove. I'll be your helper and I'll just get mummy to watch we are safe". Jamie had taken on board that two people used a bow saw, he needed a glove for his non-sawing hand and an adult to oversee the procedure. Fortunately as mum and dad had volunteered at Forest School they both new the rules and therefore dad didn't mind about mum being summoned to supervise on this occasion.

After the initial year, the project was given a further three years funding. A local further education college in Worcestershire was approached to train more leaders. The college contacted Bridgwater College and received permission to offer the BTEC leader qualification ensuring the training became sustainable in the county. This led to other sites being developed, mainly within settings. Many visitors came to Forest School at Bishops Wood Centre including the Director of Education for Worcestershire. He became a real champion of Forest School, not just in Worcestershire but in other authorities he was supporting. At a conference in 2002 he stated he wanted every foundation child in the county to have a sustained Forest School experience. This hasn't quite been achieved, but Forest School continues to flourish. In 2012 there are approximately 480 leaders in the county.

Many schools who started Forest School in Foundation Stage have now taken it throughout the primary phase because they see the benefits to their children and believe it helps to encourage positive dispositions for learning. This is borne out by the growing number of Ofsed reports that cite Forest School as helping to raise attainment.

the role of Forest School in meeting Local Authority and government key priorities i.e. raising achievement, narrowing the gap and safeguarding.

Freelance Forest School leaders

Not everyone who trains to be a Forest School leader necessarily works for an organisation and more and more people are working as freelance practitioners. This can work very well for the leader and settings. It may be the setting cannot afford to train a leader and buys someone in, or as previously mentioned, a cluster of settings can use one person between them, maximizing opportunities for sharing waterproofs, the site and sometimes transport.

Freelance leaders need a comprehensive handbook in exactly the same way as other practitioners, however they will need to add certain extras. Clients will need to know you have adequate public liability insurance; a recent enhanced criminal records bureau certificate; a current first aid certificate; a clean driving license and minibus driver's license if you are transporting children and how you will communicate with parents, staff and other adults as necessary. One freelance practitioner has drawn up a code of conduct (shared on page 77), although he rightly states:

> 'The Code is my Code – I don't mean that in terms of an issue of ownership, but that as a freelancer it is geared towards my own practice, bespoke to me. As a freelancer, clients buy you in, I think, as much for who you are (personality, interpersonal skills, experience etc) as much as the service you provide (indeed the two are inextricably interwoven). As such, reflective practice means that the Code may change as I wander along my professional journey'.

The code of conduct forms part of Mark's handbook, which contains all the necessary information a client would need such as ethos, policies procedures, risk assessments and certificates of competency.

Freelance work can be very exciting. If you take this route you may get to work on a range of different sites from woodlands to school grounds, from pocket parks to nature reserves. You can work with different age groups, different abilities, children, adults and communities. The opportunities are endless and like all Forest Schools, greatly rewarding.

CASE STUDY: OXFORDSHIRE COUNTY COUNCIL

In a similar vein to Worcestershire, senior early years managers from Oxfordshire visited Bridgwater College Forest School. On their return, a local trust that offered environmental education was contacted to see if they would be interested in managing a Forest School project in partnership with the county. A service level agreement was issued and Bridgwater College invited to deliver training.

This first cohort consisted of practitioners mainly at a managerial level and a student on teaching practice with the trust. At the end of his teacher training the student, was appointed as a part time Forest School leader for two days per week. He worked with two nursery schools and a group of pupils from a local secondary school undertaking a youth award scheme. These young people developed a site on the trusts land, a designated conservation area which had public assess. The site was fenced and a shelter and fire circle built. To discourage the public from going into the Forest School a sign was put on the gate stating 'conservation area'. The younger children were collected in a minibus and then had a ten-minute walk to the site.

After the first year, the service level agreement was extended for a further three years and leader's post was increased to full time. An early years officer with responsibility for outdoor learning was given a remit for raising awareness of Forest School within the county. A local conference was held to help disseminate information and share the results of the pilot year and further Forest School leader training offered through a local further education college. Oxford Brookes University, also working in partnership with OCC and the trust, undertook an evaluation of the project which highlighted the benefits of Forest School.

Over the period of the service level agreement the team of Forest School leaders grew to four full-time equivalent posts and other sites were sourced. One of the leaders was funded by the Early Excellence cluster, a cluster of schools all with a high number of disadvantaged children. The heads of this partnership had seen and read about the value of Forest School, in particular the benefits to

PSED and wanted to give their young children a positive learning experience. Evaluation of this pilot again proved the many advantages to giving children the opportunity to learn and thrive in a natural, outdoor environment.

A private golf club was also looking to participate in a community project and worked with a local middle school to develop a nature area on the edge of the golf course next to Oxford Brookes University. As the school closed, due to phasing out middle schools, the emergent primary school appointed a Forest School leader to develop the area further for Forest School. Again, this area was used by a cluster of schools, as well as early years students from the university, who were undertaking an outdoor learning module who used the site for practical experiences.

After a change in management at the trust, it was decided not to renew the service level agreement with the county as the trust wanted to concentrate on more formal environmental education programmes. However, the county did not wish to lose the momentum of Forest School and therefore the staff team was transferred (under TUPE) over to the county and became employees of Oxfordshire County Council who continue to support and fund a strong team.

The original leader was seconded to a local fresh start school for two days a week. He worked with children throughout the primary age giving every child in the school the opportunity of a sustained Forest School programme. As well as taking children off-site, he developed areas of the school grounds and three members of staff trained to be leaders to be able to continue Forest School after the secondment came to an end. The headteacher of this school has now moved on but has started Forest School in his new setting and hopes to follow a similar model with all children having a sustained Forest School environment. Oxfordshire is primarily a rural county but there are areas of high deprivation and also a transient community with several large barracks for forces personnel. Forest School in Oxfordshire continues to grow and bring benefits to many, many, children.
(See also page 79, Mulvany. R, 2012 unpublished.)

As you can see from the case studies, the key to their success is the having strategic officers on board. Oxfordshire and Worcestershire are not the only local authorities who support Forest School. Other authorities that have thriving Forest School programmes include

Shropshire, Norfolk, Devon, Derbyshire, Sandwell and Dudley, to name but a few.

Many government and non-government organisations throughout Great Britain also successfully support Forest School.

Code of conduct

This code of conduct briefly summarises how I will work, values and ethics. It is supported by more detailed policies and procedures in the section following this code.

1. **Compliance:** I will comply with all necessary legal requirements, for example holding a current Enhanced CRB certificate, Health and Safety regulations, Child Protection, and Public Liability Insurance.

2. **Competence:** I will hold all necessary certificates and complete training to ensure that I am competent to fulfil the work required. This would include such things as Forest School leader Level 3, Emergency First Aid as a minimum.

3. **Child Protection:** As a Creative Practitioner working with children I aim to provide activities that will encourage learning and developmental opportunities and assist them to develop new skills within a safe environment. Developing procedures and guidelines, will help to minimise the potential for abuse and create a positive environment for everyone involved.

4. **No-Harm Principle:** No activity will aim to result in harm of any sort to the participants, adults or children. This will be supported through Child Protection and Health and Safety policies and procedures.

5. **Beneficence:** Children and young people will only be invited to participate in activities where there are benefits to the experience.

6. **Mutual Trust and Respect:** I support and embrace a policy of equal opportunities. I will endeavour to develop mutual trust and respect with all participants, both children and adults, through impartiality and open and clear communication. All activities will acknowledge and promote the children's voice.

7. **Transparency:** I will aim to ensure that there is transparency in my practice, including my approach, planning and decision making through clear and open communications.

8. **Shared Authorship:** My creative practice is based on a partnership approach with the children and other practitioners. This means co-constructive learning, supporting participants to develop their own work, not imposing my ideas or outcomes on the participants, and ensuring the participants have a voice in the work.

9. **Confidentiality:** Everything is confidential. I can reveal what happens in a project if the participants, (or their parents/ guardians), consent, or if the law says I must.

10. **Consent:** People will participate only if they give their consent, without being forced, coerced or manipulated into doing so.

Reproduced with kind permission from Mark Riley, Creative-States

Research

There have been many small-scale research projects and more and more students are using Forest School as their dissertation subject. At present there is no central library for the collation of these. However this is something the new governing body is hoping to address.

One major piece of research that is available to download is: 'Such Enthusiasm – a joy to see' (Murray and O'Brien 2005); an evaluation of Forest School in England. The evaluation draws out the main key features and themes of Forest School, below.

Key features of Forest School

- **The use of a woodland setting** framed by strict safety routines and established boundaries that allows the flexibility and freedom for child-initiated learning and other innovative approaches to learning to take place in a low-risk environment.

- **A high adult to pupil ratio** allows for children to undertake tasks and play activities that challenge them but do not put them at undue risk of harm.

- **Learning can be linked** to the National Curriculum and Foundation Stage objectives whilst setting those objectives in a different context – and it is not focused just on the natural environment.

- **The freedom to explore using multiple senses** is fundamental for encouraging creative, diverse and imaginative play.

- **Regular contact for the children** over a significant period of time at least one morning, afternoon or day per week from six to twelve months or more.

Key evaluation themes

Themes 1 to 6 below relate to the impact of Forest School on the children studied. Themes 7 and 8 are concerned with the wider impacts of Forest School on parents and teachers.

1. **Confidence** – This was characterised by self-confidence and self-belief that came from the children having the freedom, time and space, to learn, grown and demonstrate independence.

2. **Social skills** – The children demonstrated an increased awareness of the consequences of their actions on other people, peers and adults, and acquired a better ability to work co-operatively with others.

3. **Language and communication** – The children developed more sophisticated uses of both written and spoken language prompted by their visual and sensory experiences at Forest School.

4. **Motivation and concentration** – This was characterised by a keenness to participate in exploratory learning and play activities as well as the ability to focus on specific tasks for extended periods of time.

5. **Physical skills** – The children developed physical stamina and their gross motor skills through free and easy movement round the Forest School site. They developed fine motor skills by making objects and structures.

6. **Knowledge and understanding** – Increased respect for the environment was developed as well as an interest in their natural surroundings. Observational improvements were noted as the children started to identify flora and fauna.

7. **New perspectives** – The teachers and practitioners gained a new perspective and understanding of the children as they observed them in a very different setting and were able to identify their individual learning styles.

8. **Ripple effects beyond Forest School** – The children brought their experience home and asked their parents to take them outdoors at the weekend or in the school holidays. Parents' interest and attitude towards Forest School changed as they saw the impacts on their children.

This research, along with an earlier evaluation 'A study in Wales' was funded by The Forestry Commission (available from www.forestry.gov.uk/fr/INFD-6HKEMH).

Raising achievement

In Oxfordshire, a piece of action research mapped the possible effectiveness of Forest School in relation to three county council priorities: raising achievement, narrowing the gap and keeping children safe–along with two curriculum areas in which Oxfordshire falls below the national average; communication, language and literacy and personal, social and emotional development. Summary statements from the study affirmed that Forest School does impact on all the areas analysed and this is beginning to be borne out by the many Ofsted reports citing Forest School as being instrumental in raising achievement.

Evidence was found to support the claim that Forest School is effective at raising achievement. All of the staff involved in the study reported Forest School as having a very positive effect on their groups, and analysis of EYFSP scores has shown how important Forest School was to the children. In many instances there were profile scores that children were able to achieve only because of their Forest School experiences.

At Forest School, children are most predisposed to learn; they are engaged, motivated and confident. The learning that occurs is of great value, and adds enormously to the children's learning in all areas.

It was clear from the evidence collected during this study that Forest School offers the children something special, something unique that would be very difficult to replicate elsewhere in school (Mulvany. R, 2010 unpublished).

Quality Improvement Framework (QIF)

As the numbers of Forest School leaders and Forest School sites began to grow in Worcestershire, the need for some sort of quality benchmark was identified. Several quality frameworks were investigated and as Worcestershire practitioners were familiar with Accounting Early for Lifelong Learning (AcE), it was decided to develop a similar robust self-assessment document relating to Forest School, which encouraged a rigorous and continuous culture of evaluation. Several workshops were held with practitioners to tease out the bones of what was required and over the course of a year the flesh was added and the document written.

At the same time, the Forestry Commission was also looking at options for a Quality Assurance mark for Forest School and so the two organisations worked together to refine the document and match it to quality indicators. The resulting Quality Improvement Framework (QIF) is a comprehensive self-evaluation tool. It offers a continuous and ongoing journey of improvement to practice whilst tracking progress and providing rigorous evidence of outcomes for children.

of reference with evidence collated all in one place as a communication tool. The QIF is available for all practitioners (download from www.foresteducation.org/forestschool).

Continuing professional development (CPD)

Most Forest School trainers and other environmental trainers offer a selection of CPD courses. These may be of a practical nature such as tool skills, fire lighting or cooking, creative such as storymaking or whittling and theoretical, for example emotional intelligence or managing challenging behaviour. Like any qualification, Forest School is the start of a learning journey that benefits from wider ongoing training, depending on needs of the practitioner, their learners and of course personal interests.

Examples of courses:

- Working with Challenging Behaviour in the Outdoors (OCN Level 3)

- Storymaking and storytelling at Forest School

- Whittling in the woods

- Making safe play structures

- Fires and fire lighting methods

- Emotional literacy in the outdoors

- First aid in the outdoors.

Evidence of this kind is essential for Local Authorities or other funding bodies and to ensure children have the best possible experience whilst at Forest School. Four quality indicators cover the key areas of Forest School: The Learning Environment, Health, Safety and Well-being, Delivery and Communication and Learners. For each of the four Quality Indicator areas, there is a self-evaluation checklist. This consists of a question, suggested evidence, own evidence and action points. The format has been developed in a way that it can be worked through as section at a time. Measuring quality can be extremely difficult with an experiential programme such as Forest School. However using a tool such as the QIF can highlight the many areas of good practice as well as areas for improvement and tracking progress.

Several local authorities, including Worcestershire, Shropshire and Oxfordshire use the QIF as their benchmark for quality and it can be used as evidence towards other organisational national requirements such as the 'Learning Outside the Classroom' quality mark.

Although there isn't a nationally recognised 'badge' for completing the Forest School QIF, practitioners who have undertaken this have commented how valuable it is, not only to reflect on their own practice, but to have a source

Food hygiene certificate

All practitioners who handle food, whether it is indoors or out of doors, are required to have at least a basic food hygiene certificate. If you are cooking on a fairly regular basis then a Level 2 hygiene certificate is the one to go for. These courses are readily available online and are not very expensive. The revised Statutory Framework for the EYFS clearly states: "*In group provision, all staff involved in preparing and handling food must receive training in food hygiene*" (DfE, 2012, p.22). One person should have a HACCP, Hazard and Critical Control Point, which looks at the risk of buying, transporting and handling food.

Cooking over the campfire with young children is hugely rewarding and well worth the effort. Try to think more creatively than marshmallows. Damper bread is often a good starter as are pancakes and dropscones. Quesadillas, chapatis, bannock bread, falafel and soup are quick and easy to make. This is a really good opportunity to look at cultural and global aspects and attributes.

National Governing Body

It has long been recognised that the Forest School movement needs a more formal organisation to represent the needs of practitioners and act as a voice to influence policy. Since 2002 there have been various attempts at bringing together the Forest School community. In 2008 several Forest School practitioners met with a representative from the Institute of Outdoor Learning (IOL), an organisation with a good track record in the outdoor learning world. Although traditionally IOL have represented the more 'hard' skills such as rock climbing, canoeing and potholing, they were interested in embracing 'soft' skills. IOL had started some special interest groups under their umbrella and it was felt this would be a good starting point for a Forest School national body.

In September 2008 the IOL Forest School Special Interest Group (FSSIG) was launched with a membership of approximately 60. This has grown to approximately 270 in 2012. The group has an elected executive committee and a constitution. IOL looked after the monies raised from membership and conferences and host a dedicated area for the Forest School SIG on their website.

In 2010 the IOL FSSIG organised their first conference with Richard Louv, author of *Last Child in the Wood*, as the guest speaker attracting an audience of 200 delegates and in 2011 a second conference was held with Sue Palmer and Sara Knight as key note speakers again with attendance in the 100's.

Although this group was thriving it was still felt the Forest School movement should work towards the formation of a National Governing Body. IOL, FSSIG and the Forest School Training Network (FSTN) worked together to achieve this goal through a small working party. Monies raised through the conferences and grant funding enabled a development officer to be appointed on a one year contract, to prepare

a business plan through consultation with the wider Forest School community. The development officer was employed by IOL and the process recorded through the posting of meeting minutes on the Forest School page of the website. The overwhelming evidence from all the consultations was that the Forest School movement should have its own governing body to represent the interests of the very diverse community.

So where are we now?

On July 7th 2012 some 200 of the Forest School community, from all parts of the UK, came together at Elvason Castle Country Park in Derby to launch the new Forest School National Governing Body.

A Forest School timeline was presented (see page 89) and some 180 people registered to join the organization for a nominal fee of £20. We sat in the grounds of the castle where members were bought up to date with consultation process, how the future organization would be organised and the makeup of the board of directors. A vote was taken to appoint the executive members of the board and there was a debate on the name of the new organisation.

Tim Gill, the honoury role of patron to the new association, sent a welcoming message which was read to the delegates. As part of this message Tim said:

> "*For me, the potential of Forest School is built on two vital foundation stones: the intrinsic qualities of natural places, and the intrinsic motivations and learning impulses of children. If Forest School is to leave a lasting impression on the lives of the children and young people who experience it, these two need equal emphasis.*"

(To read the full version of Tim's message go to http://rethinkingchildhood.com/2012/07/09/outdoor-learning/#more-2001)

It was felt the time was right to revise the definition and principles that had been adopted in 2002 and this reviewed ethos, and the principles and criteria were arrived at after consultation with the Forest School community by the Forest School Institute for Outdoor Learning Special Interest Group, the Forest School GB Trainers Network and Forest School NGB working group in 2011. They were pulled together by the FS NGB Development Officer during 2011/2012 and published in February 2012.

Ethos/Definition

> "*Forest School is an inspirational process that offers ALL learners regular opportunities to achieve, develop confidence and self-esteem, through hands on learning experiences in a local woodland or natural environment with trees.*"

Forest School is a specialised approach that sits within and compliments the wider context of outdoor and woodland learning.

Principles with criteria for good practice (FS = Forest School)

1. **Forest School is a long-term process with frequent and regular sessions in a local natural space, not a one-off visit. Planning, adaption, observations and reviewing are integral elements.**

- FS takes place regularly, ideally at least every other week, over an extended period of time, if practicable encompassing the seasons.

- A FS programme has a structure which is based on the observations and joint work between learners and practitioners. This structure should clearly demonstrate progression of learning.

- The initial sessions of any programme establish physical and behavioural boundaries as well as making initial observations on which to base future programme development.

2. **Forest School takes place in a woodland or natural wooded environment to support the development of a relationship between the learner and the natural world.**

- Whilst woodland is the ideal environment for FS, many other sites, some with only a few trees, are able to support good FS practice.

- The woodland is ideally suited to match the needs of the programme and learners, providing them with the space and environment in which to explore and discover.

- A FS programme constantly monitors its ecological impact and works within a sustainable site management plan agreed between the landowner/manager and the practitioner and the learners.

- FS aims to foster a relationship with nature through regular personal experiences in a local woodland/wooded site to help develop long term environmentally sustainable attitudes and practices in staff, learners and the wider community.

- FS uses the natural resources for inspiration, to enable ideas and encourage intrinsic motivation.

3. **Forest School aims to promote the holistic development of all those involved, fostering resilient, confident, independent and creative learners.**

- Where appropriate the FS leader will aim to link experiences at FS to home, work and/or school/education.

- FS programmes aim to develop, where appropriate, the physical, social, cognitive, linguistic, emotional, social and spiritual aspects of the learner.

4. **Forest School offers learners the opportunity to take supported risks appropriate to the environment and themselves.**

- FS opportunities are designed to build on an individual's innate motivation, positive attitudes and/or interests.

- FS uses tools and fires only where deemed appropriate to the learners, and is dependent on completion of a baseline risk assessment.

- Any FS experience follows a risk/benefit process managed jointly by the practitioner and learner that is tailored to the developmental stage of the learner.

5. **Forest School is run by qualified Forest School practitioners who continuously develop their professional practice.**

- FS is led by qualified Forest School practitioners, who are required to hold a minimum of an equivalent Level 3 qualification.

- There is a high practitioner/adults to learner ratio.

- Practitioners and adults regularly helping at Forest School are subject to relevant checks into their suitability to have prolonged contact with children, young people and vulnerable people.

- Practitioners need to hold an up to date first aid qualification which includes paediatric and outdoor elements.

- FS is backed by relevant working documents which contain all the relevant policies and procedures required for running FS and establish the roles and responsibilities of staff and volunteers.

- The FS leader is a reflective practitioner sees themselves as a learner too.

6. **Forest School uses a range of learner-centred processes to create a community for development and learning.**

- A learner-centred pedagogical approach is employed that is responsive to the needs and interests of the learners.

- Play and choice are an integral part of the FS learning process and play is recognised as vital to learning and development at FS.

- FS provides a stimulus for all learning preferences and dispositions.

- Reflective practice is a feature of each session to ensure learners and practitioners can understand their achievements, develop emotional intelligence and plan for the future.

- Practitioner observation is an important element of FS pedagogy. Observations are used to 'scaffold' and tailor learning and development at FS.

- The practitioner models the pedagogy which they promote during their programmes through careful planning, appropriate dialogue and relationship building.

Further information can be found on the IOL website on page 95.

Conclusion

By author Jenny Doyle

As I start to enter a new phase in my life and think about retirement, it is a good time to reflect upon over 40 years of working with children in a wide range of settings in the voluntary, private and maintained sectors, within education and health services. I can honestly say the last twelve years, working in Forest School, have been the happiest and most rewarding of my whole career. I have been fortunate enough to visit Demark and Finland, have travelled to Northern Ireland, Wales and all over England to see, share and join in with Forest School.

I have met amazing and passionate practitioners who are giving children, young people and adults the most wonderful experiences on a regular basis. I have seen how Forest School training has impacted on practitioner's wider practice and how parents, carers, grandparents, caretakers and volunteers have embraced this way of learning. For many it has taken them back to their own childhood. For others it has given them a sense of freedom and well-being that only regular contact with nature can provide. This is being reinforced by recent research and movements like the 'Children and Nature' network (http://www.childrenandnature.org) and the Forest School Association – championed by those such as Tim Gill, Richard Louv and Marjory Ouvry to name but a few.

But most of all I have gained such a lot from the children. The awe and wonder, their curiosity, their ingenuity, the enthusiasm (no matter what the weather) and the depth of learning and problem solving I have observed have been a privilege to witness. I have gained more than I have given and I thank all of those children for sharing their explorations with me.

I urge anyone reading this book to train, at whichever Level is suitable, and become involved with Forest School. Forest School really does make a difference to raising achievement and we owe it to our children and ourselves to get outside more into woodlands and natural areas and see the spontaneous learning that takes place.

By author Katherine Milchem

Colleagues and I have been astonished by almighty nature and its altering effects our experiences have had on children and adults. We were not prepared by how motivating and powerful a natural environment would be for promoting creativity, talk, rich and meaningful learning opportunities and collaborative activity.

We have all experienced how being out in nature uplifts our moods, makes us feel more alert and opens our air passages. The calmness freshen our minds and spirits. All of the children have progressed in very individual ways and the environment has helped adults become more reflective practitioners who are in-tune with the children's needs and interests.

Developing a Forest School programme is an evolutionary process for both adults and the children. Just as children and adults develop in individual ways and rates, so will Forest School provisions in different settings.

As Forest School practitioners and staff gain more experience working with groups outdoors, they will discover what works and what does not, they will become more confident in their skills and in planning experiences tailored to the group. Reflective practice and continuing professional development will refine and further improve their practice. Regular exposure to natural environments will help children become more confident and as they acquire skills they will show more independence in leading and controlling their learning and will attempt increasingly challenging activities.

Within this book, it has not been possible to cover everything involved in setting up a Forest School. The journey taken by the staff to setting up programmes in a variety of early years settings will be individual and unique. However, we hope we have provided you with a base to get started.

Through my own journey, I have discovered that there is no definite way of setting up or delivering Forest School. Something that is possible in one setting may not be in another. Every Forest School will be unique, as it is a reflection of its children, families and staff. I have found that it is important to share with other professionals the bespoke qualities of our Forest School programme, whilst maintaining an open-minded approach to the ways Forest School ethos is being embraced in their settings. I have learnt a lot from practice taking place in other settings.

Hopefully Forest Schools will continue to spread and new provisions will form and grow. If they do, they will be extending the reach of what is most children's preferred learning environment (the great outdoors!).

Jenny and I have shared examples of good early years practice which embodies Forest School ethos. We hope that by sharing the knowledge, skills and experience gained through our Forest School journeys, we will encourage others to share, learn from and reflect on the practice in their setting and in others.

IF...

If I can
ask my own questions,

try out my ideas

experience what's around me,

share what I find;

If I have

Plenty of time for my special place,

a nourishing space,

things to transform;

If you'll be

my patient friend,

my trusted guide,

fellow investigator,

partner in learning;

Then I will

Explore the world,

discover my voice

and tell you what I know

in a hundred languages.

(Written by Pamela Houk with suggestions from Lella Gandini and the late Loris Malaguzzi)

Children Learn what they Live

If children live with criticism, they learn to condemn.

If children live with hostility, they learn to fight.

If children live with fear, they learn to be apprehensive.

If children live with pity, they learn to feel sorry for themselves.

If children live with ridicule, they learn to feel shy.

If children live with jealousy, they learn to feel envy.

If children live with shame, they learn to feel guilty.

If children live with encouragement, they learn confidence.

If children live with tolerance, they learn patience.

If children live with praise, they learn appreciation.

If children live with acceptance, they learn to love.

If children live with approval, they learn to like themselves.

If children live with recognition, they learn it is good to have a goal.

If children live with sharing, they learn generosity.

If children live with honesty, they learn truthfulness.

If children live with fairness, they learn justice.

If children live with kindness and consideration, they learn respect.

If children live with security, they learn to have faith in themselves and in those about them.

If children live with friendliness, they learn the world is a nice place in which to live.

Copyright © 1972 by Dorothy Law Nolte

Eastwood Nursery Forest School Session Plan		Date:	Weather:
Group:	Leader and staff:	Parent/Guardian/Visitor:	

Mark making with mud, making tree faces/spirits

Previous experience/knowledge: Children have had opportunities to play with clay and combine it with natural objects in the setting. Most of the group will not have heard of tree faces/spirits (e.g. Green Man) or have had the experience of working with clay in a natural environment.

Objectives/Learning outcomes (30-50 months and 40-60 months)

Personal Social and Emotional – work as part of a group or class, take turns, show confidence linking up with others, talk about emotions (on faces).

Personal Social and Emotional and Physical Development – appreciate the need for hygiene, show independence getting ready/undressed.

Understanding the World – build and construct with purpose using a wide range of objects, selecting resources and adapting their work, talk about what is seen and changes in the environment.

Mathematics – use math language (sizes and weight), discuss shape, use positional language.

Expressive Arts and Design – understand that different media can be combined to create new effects, talk about personal intentions.

Physical Development – understand that equipment and tools have to be used safely. Experiment with movements.

Communication and Language – storytelling, communicate needs and wishes, interact with others, negotiate, plan activities/make marks.

IEP considerations/adaptations: simplified language, visual prompts and gesturing for children with EAL.

Exploring Schemas:	Engaging learning styles:
In/out/going through Enveloping	Visual – 1, 2 Come along with me, 3, 4 and What do you see?
Containing/enclosure Transporting	Auditory – 1, 2 Come very near, 3, 4 and What do you hear?
Containing/enclosure Trajectory Connection Containing/enclosure	Kinaesthetic – 1, 2, Come let's kneel, 3, 4 and What do you feel?

Activities	Resources	Vocabulary
1. **Getting Ready, brief group** (including parents/visitors). 2. **Safety talk, walk to site** (sing 'Here we go to FS' and 'Stop Look Listen Road Safety' songs). 3. **Revisit rules/boundaries for safety and behaviour.** 4. **Free exploration in the environment.** 5. **Small achievable task** – Talk about tree spirits and faces. Choose a tree you like and decorate it with mud paintings and or create a tree face/spirit out of clay. 6. **Go to base camp, fold out ground sheet.** 7. **Elder Cordial/water and healthy snack** – hygiene, sharing. 8. **Play safety game** (one, two, three, Where are you?) or hide and seek (find each other by voice/sound direction). 9. **Tidy up** (Song: 'Clean up, clean up, everybody, everywhere, clean up, clean up everybody do your share!'). 10. **Circle time reflection and planning next session, Walking back** (Who? What did you see, hear, touch, smell? Which?, How?, commenting 'I wonder if…' I think…').	Clothing and rucksack, camera, dictaphone, mobile phone, tissues, first aid kit, spare clothes; free exploration; formation, revisit rules, only pick things off the ground, do not put anything near/in mouth, stay together, walk on bumpy path. Find a tree, identify it using a book/sheets, photos of tree spirits (Green man), clay, tools, mats, natural objects, water (in a bottle) paint trays and brushes to make marks on trees with mud; water flask, fruit, cups, hand sanitiser, wet wipes, Elderflower cordial; open questions, voice of child, evaluation/planning.	Weather, together, hold hands, safe, help, pedestrian crossing, green man, red man, traffic light; mix, paint, draw, mark, write, find, collect, clay stick, mould, emotions, size and weight; texture words: clean, rub, germs, sip/cool/taste, healthy, energy. One, two, three, Where are you? Listen, respond, voice, direction; tidy up, clean respect; likes/dislikes

Session number	Title of session	Aims	Resources	Activity overview
1	Collecting bag	Seek and delight in new experiences / Explore and experience using a range of senses	Paper, stapler, string, masking tape	123 games, collecting materials for introduction to environment and discussion
2	Texture challenge	Notice differences in features of the local environment / Make comparisons and create new connections	String, scissors	123 games, collect items of interesting texture, attach to string and in group make shower curtain
3	Sticky crowns	Begin to use talk to pretend imaginary situations / Describe and talk about what they see	Strips of paper with double sided sticky tape. Book (Deep in a rainforest)	Collect items in a variety of colours and stick to tape, fire safety game
4	Minibeast hunt	Show care and concern for others, living things and the environment / Find out about their environment, and talk about those features they like and dislike	Collecting pots, plastic spoons, magnifying glasses, reference sheet	Minibeast collecting in pots using spoons, fire safety game
5	Mud hedgehogs	Show willingness to get dirty / Talk activities through, reflecting on and modifying what they are doing / Working cooperatively in a group	Lots of water and garden tools	Fire safety game including collecting materials, make mud and create hedgehogs etc
6	Real fire and hot drinks	Listen to instructions and follow safety guidelines / Use talk and action to recall and relive past experiences	Chocolate powder, fire striker, cotton wool, Kelly kettle	Collect fire materials, start fire, make hot chocolate
Health and safety		Leading adult is always at the front when entering copse of trees and assesses for any dangers taking action as necessary. Children are warned about any possible dangers and are introduced to rules and 123 games during first session. There will always be a named first aider who will carry any medicines and all consent/medical forms.		
Equal opportunities		All children are given the opportunity to take part in forest school. Children are grouped thoughtfully giving each child the maximum potential to develop new skills and succeed in all activities.		
Self esteem		Children are offered the chance to try new things and speak in the group but not pressured if they do not feel ready. Children are taught the rules and encouraged to ask questions and voice their opinions if they need more clarification or wish to discuss something.		
Independence		Children are taught rules and allowed to question and discuss those rules. Children are encouraged to be independent that they are ready for in all activities, adults are always on hand to offer guidance but children are encouraged to do for themselves where they can.		
Schema		Connection/joining, enveloping, enclosure, rotation, transporting, trajectory.		

This timeline was presented to delegates at the launch of the Forest School Association at Elvaston Castle, Derbyshire, on 7th July 2012.

1993   Bridgwater College Early Years students visit to Denmark

1994   Bridgwater Early Excellence start Forest School on the college grounds

1995   Bridgwater College develop the Edexel BTEC qualification

2002   First National Forest School Conference at Bishops Wood Centre Worcestershire

FEI, England coordinator seconded to map Forest School and create practitioner data base.
Forest School, England, Network created. Unelected committee formed

2003   OCN training units developed in Wales

2006   Forest School trainers' network formed for Wales

2007   England trainers' join Wales Network

2008   13th May Proposal for create Institute of Outdoor learning (IOL) Forest School Special Interest Group (FS SIG) by Forest School England Network

2008   20th September Launch of the IOL FS FIG at Bromsgrove, Worcestershire

Elected executive committee formed

2008   England Forest School trainers' network established

2009   21st November 1st IOL FS SIG AGM at Oxford – majority vote to pursue establishment of national governing body (NGB) – working group formed

2010   On line consultation about formation of NGB from June to September

2010   5th June IOL FS SIG conference – Worcester University – keynote speaker Richard Louv, author of 'Last Child in the Woods'

2010   13th November, 2nd IOL FS SIG AGM at Roehampton University, London

2010   Funding secured to recruit development officer to write business plan for proposed NGB

2011   February – NGB development officer recruited for one year

2011   March – FEI Scotland Forest School Coordinator appointed

2011   8th October – 2nd IOL FS SIG Conference and 3rd AGM – Liddington PGL Centre, Swindon – key note speakers Sue Palmer and Sara Knight, authors

2011   15th October – On-line consultation on revised Forest School Principles

2012   March – Forest School business plan circulated

2012   1st May – consultation on dissolution of IOL FS SIG

2012   3rd May – online consultation on name and board representation of new association

2012   11th May – invitation to Forest School community to the launch of the new association

2012   7th July – LAUNCH of new association at Elvaston Castle, Derbyshire

Forest School Association Inauguration

Elected officers for Board of Directors

And for the future (at the time of printing)

2012   IOL FS SIG AGM – October, possible dissolution

2012   Appointment of development officer for new Forest School Association

2013   6th July Forest School Association AGM and conference

References

Articles and policies

Bentsen, P., Søndergaard Jensen, F., Mygind, E., and Barfoed Randrup, T. (2010) The extent and dissemination of udeskole in Danish schools. *Urban Forestry and Urban Greening* 1-9. Website: http://www.udeskole.dk/media/bentsen%20etal%20the%20extent%20and%20dissemination%20of%20udeskole%20in%20Danish%20schools%20in%20press.pdf (accessed 06/06/2011).

Clark, A and Moss, P. (2001) *Listening to young children: the Mosaic approach*, National Children's Bureau, London.

Clark, A and Moss, P. (2005) *Spaces to Play: more listening to young children using the Mosaic approach*, London.

David, A. (2010) *Fundraising: A step-by-step guide to fundraising for your early years setting*, Practical Pre-School Books, London.

Defries, M. (2009) 'Outdoors Can Beat the Indoors for Learning', *Nursery World*.
Website: http://www.nurseryworld.co.uk/news/969124/Outdoors-beat-indoors-learning-conference-told/ (accessed 27/02/2010).

Department for Education (2012) Early Years Foundation Stage. Website: http://www.education.gov.uk/schools/teachingandlearning/curriculum/a0068102/early-years-foundation-stage-eyfs

Department for Environment Food and Rural Affairs (DEFRA). (2011) *The Natural Choice: securing the value of nature*, The Stationary Office, London. Website: http://www.defra.gov.uk

DfES (2006) *Learning Outside the Classroom Manifesto*, HMSO (and www.lotc.org.uk), Nottingham.

Eastwood Nursery School Centre For Children and Families – Urban Forest School website: www.urbanforestschool.co.uk

Every Child Matters: https://www.education.gov.uk/publications

Gill, T. (2010) 'Nothing Ventured… Balancing risks and benefits in the outdoors', English Outdoor Council.

Gulløv, E. (2003) 'Creating a natural place for children: an enthnographic study of Danish Kindergartens' in Fog Olwig K., and Gulløv, E. (eds.) *Children's Places: cross cultural perspectives*, Routledge, London.

Her Majesty's Inspectors (HMI) (2008) *Learning Outside the Classroom: How Far Should You Go?*, Ofsted, London. http://www.ofsted.gov.uk

House of Commons, Children, Schools and Families Committee. (2009-2010) *Transforming Education Outside the Classroom*, The Stationary Office, London. http://www.publications.parliament.uk/pa/cm200910/cmselect/cmchilsch/418/418.pdf (accessed 22/06/2011).

Murrey, R. and O'Brian, L. (2005) *Such Enthusiasm – a joy to see*. Report to the Forestry Commission by New Economics Foundation and Forest Research.

O'Brien, L. and Murray, R. (2006) *A marvellous opportunity for children to learn: a participatory evaluation of Forest School in England and Wales*, Forest Research, Norwich.

Swarbrick, N., Eastwood, G., and Tutton, K. (2004) 'Self-esteem and successful interaction as part of the Forest School project', *Support for Learning* 19(3),142-146.

Pound, L (2008) *How children learn*, Practical Pre-School Books, London.

Pound, L. (2009) *How children learn 3: Contemporary thinking and theorists*, Practical Pre-School Books, London.

For information on the Edexcel BTEC Forest School leader award contact www.bridgwater.ac.uk

Further resources

Books

Below is a useful selection of books for adults and children to support play and learning outdoors.

Children's books

Minibeasts:

Donaldson, J. (2012) *Superworm*, Alison Green Books, London.

Carle, E. (2000) *The Bad-tempered Ladybird*, Puffin, London.

Carle, E. (1996) *The Very Busy Spider*, Hamish Hamilton, Harmondsworth.

Carle, E. (1970) *The Very Hungry Caterpillar*, Hamilton, London.

Monks, L. (2006) *Aaaarrgghh Spider*, Egmont, London.

Langham, T. (2008) *Creepy Crawly Calypso*, Massachusetts, Barefoot Books.

Imaginary creatures and objects:

Donaldson, J. (2011) *Freddie and the Fairy*, Macmillan, London.

Donaldson, J. (1999) *The Gruffalo*, Macmillan, London.

Donaldson, J. (2004) *The Gruffalo's Child*, Macmillan, London.

Donaldson, J. (2009) *Stick Man*, Alison Green Books, London.

Hegley, J. (2012) *Stanley's Stick*, Hodder Children's Books, London.

Sharratt, N. (2008) *The Foggy, Foggy Forest*, Walker, London.

Willis, J. (2008) *The Bog Baby*, Puffin, London.

Life cycles:

Carle, E. (2000) *The Very Hungry Caterpillar*, Hamish Hamilton, London.

Carle, E. (2009) *The Tiny Seed*, Simon and Schuster, London.

Halliday, N. (2005) *The Lonely Tree*, Halliday Slough.

Parsons, R. (2005) *Harry's Hazelnut*, Storysack Ltd, Bury.

Seasons and weather:

Butterworth, N. (1992) *After the Storm*, HarperCollins, London.

Butterworth, N. (1995) *A Year in Percy's Park*, Collins, London.

Cowley, J. (2008) *Mrs Wishy-Washy*, Philomel Books.

Cunliffe, J. (1982) *The Foggy Day*, Andre Deutsch, London.

Dodds, S. (2002) *My World, My Seasons*, Watts, London.

Hutchins, P. (1994) *The Wind Blew*, Red Fox, London.

Keats, E.J. (1976) *The Snowy Day*, Penguin, New York.

McKee, D. (2007) *Elmer and the Rainbow*, Andersen Press, London.

McKee, D. (1994) *Elmer's Weather*, Andersen Press, London.

McKee, D. (1999) *Elmer in the Snow*, Red Fox, London.

McKee, D. (1999) *Elmer And The Wind*, Red Fox, London.

Nelson, R. (2008) *First Step Weather: A Cloudy Day*, Lerner.

Wells, R. (2004) *Ruby's Rainy Day*, Grosset and Dunlap.

Further resources

Animals:

Brett, J. (1990) *The Mitten*, Simon and Schuster, London.

Browne, A. and Friends, (2010) *Bear's Magic Pencil*, HarperCollins, London.

Corderoy, T. (2010) *The Little White Owl*, Little Tiger Press, London.

Donaldson, J. (2002) *Night Monkey Day Monkey*, Egmont London.

Donaldson, J. (2008) *One Mole Digging a Hole*, Macmillan, London.

Hopgood, T. (2009) *Wow Said the Owl*, Macmillan, London.

Griffiths, N. (2002) *Itchy Bear*, Storysack, Bury.

James, S. (2005) *Dear Greenpeace*, Walker, London.

Lloyd, S. (2008) *Wendy the Wide Mouthed Frog*, Templar, Dorking.

Prescott, S. (2009) *On a Dark Dark Night*, Little Tiger Press, London.

Root, P. (2003) *Oliver Finds His Way*, Walker, London.

Terry, M. (2012) *Who Lives Here?*, Bloomsbury, London.

Tomlinson, J. and Howard, P. (2005) *The Owl Who Was Afraid Of The Dark*, Egmont, London.

Rosen, M. (2005) *We're Going on a Bear Hunt*, Walker Books, London.

Waddell, M.(2006) *Owl Babies*, Walker, London.

Watt, M. (2008) *The Scaredy Squirrel*, Happy Cat, London.

Adult books on Forest School:

Constable, K. (2012) *The Outdoor Classroom Ages 3-7: Using Ideas from Forest Schools to Enrich Learning*, Routledge, Oxon.

Knight, S. (2011) *Forest School For All*, SAGE, London; Los Angeles.

Knight, S. (2009) *Forest Schools and Outdoor Learning in the Early Years*, SAGE, London.

Knight, S. (2011) *Risk and Adventure in Outdoor Play: Learning from Forest Schools*, SAGE, Los Angeles.

Warden, C. (2010) *Nature kindergartens: an exploration on naturalistic learning within nature kindergartens and Forest Schools*, Mindstretchers, Scotland.

Williams-Siegfredsen, J. (2012) *Understanding the Danish Forest School Approach: Early Years Education in Practice*, Routledge, Oxon.

Reference books on British nature:

Chinery, M. (2009) *Collins Complete Guide – British Insects: A photographic guide to every common species*, Collins, London.

de la Bedoyere, C. (2008) *British Wildlife Detectives' Handbook*, Miles Kelly, London.

de la Bedoyere, C. (2008) *Tree Detectives' Handbook*, Miles Kelly, London.

Moss, S. (2009) *The Bumper Book of Nature*, Square Peg, London.

Sterry, P. (2008) *Collins Complete Guide – British Wildlife: A photographic guide to every common species*, Collins, London.

Sterry, P. (2008) *Collins Complete Guide – British Wild Flowers: A photographic guide to every common species*, Collins, London.

Further resources

Sterry, P. (2008) *Collins Complete Guide – British Trees: A photographic guide to every common species*, Collins, London.

Sterry, P. (2008) *Collins Complete British Mushrooms and Toadstools: The essential photograph guide to Britain's fungi*, Collins, London.

Sterry, P. (2008) *Collins Complete Guide – British Birds: A photographic guide to every common species*, Collins, London.

Taylor, B. (2005) *Nature Detectives' Handbook*, Miles Kelly, London.

Outdoor play and research:

Austin, R. (2007) *Letting the Outside in: Developing Teaching and Learning Beyond the Early Years Classroom*, Trentham, Stoke-on-Trent.

Bilton, H. (2010) *Outdoor Learning in the Early Years: Management and Innovation*, Routledge, Oxon.

Bruce, T. (Editor) (2012) *Early Childhood Practice: Froebel today*, SAGE, London.

Davis, J. (2010) *Young Children and the Environment Early Education for Sustainability*, Cambridge University Press.

Goddard Blythe, S. (2011) *The Genius of Natural Childhood: Secrets of Thriving Children*, Hawthorn Press.

Harriman, H. (2008) *The Outdoor Classroom: A Place to Learn*, Red Robin Books, London.

Louv, R. (2008) *The Last Child In the Woods: Saving Our Children From Nature Deficit Disorder*, Chapel Hill, N.C: Algonquin Books of Chapel Hill.

Palmer, S. (2006) Toxic Childhood, Orion, London.

Ryder-Richardson, G. (1990) *Creating a Space to Grow*, Letts, London.

Schweizer, S. (2009) *Under the Sky: Playing, Working and Enjoying Adventures in the Open Air: A Handbook for Parents, Carers and Teachers*, Rudolf Steiner Press.

Tovey, H. (2007) *Playing Outdoors: Spaces and Places, Risk and Challenge*, Open University Press, Maidenhead.

Warden, C. (2007) *Nurture Through Nature*, Mindstretchers, Scotland.

White, J. (2011) *Outdoor provision in the Early Years*, SAGE, London.

White, J. (2007) *Playing and Learning Outdoors: Making Provision for High Quality Experiences in the Outdoor Environment*, The Nursery World/Routledge, London.

Books containing activities to do with children:

Cornell, J (1999) *Sharing Nature With Children: 20th Anniversary Edition: The Classic Parents' and Teachers' Nature Awareness Guidebook Revised and Expanded*, Dawn Publications, Nevada.

Danks, F. and Jo Schofield (2010) *Make it Wild!: 101 Things to Make and Do Outdoors*, Frances Lincoln, London.

Danks, F. and Jo Schofield (2009) *Go Wild!: 101 Things To Do Outdoors Before You Grow Up*, Frances Lincoln, London.

Danks, F. and Jo Schofield (2006) *Nature's Playground: Activities, Crafts and Games to Encourage Children to get Outdoors*, Frances Lincoln, London.

Danks, F. (2012) *The Stick Book: Loads of things you can make or do with a stick*, Frances Lincoln, London.

Featherstone, S. (2003) *The Little Book of Growing Things*, Featherstone Education.

Featherstone, S. (2005) *The Little Book of Living Things*, Featherstone Education.

Further resources

Featherstone, S. (2003) *The Little Book of Investigations*, Featherstone Education.

Brunton, P. and Thornton, L. (2003) *The Little Book of Light and Shadow: Little Books With Big Ideas*, Featherstone Education.

Featherstone, S. (2010) *The Little Book of Explorations*, Featherstone Education.

Holland, C. (2012) *I Love My World*, Wholeland Press, Otterton, England.

Howe, A. (1990) *Play Using Natural Materials*, Letts.

Websites

Information, reference material, nature based resources and activities: Nature Detectives (Woodland Trust): http://www.naturedetectives.org.uk/

BBC Breathing Places: http://www.bbc.co.uk/breathingplaces/schools/

Field Studies Council Open Air Laboratories: http://www.opalexplorenature.org/KidsZone

Forest School Wales: http://www.forestschoolwales.org.uk

Woodland Trust: http://www.british-trees.com/treeguide (British tree identification and resources).

The National Wildlife Federation: http://www.nwf.org (For the benefits of playing with dirt, search the website for the document: 'The Dirt on Dirt').

Eastwood Nursery School's Forest School website: www.urbanforestschool.co.uk (Information, activities and links to other websites).

RHS School Gardening: http://apps.rhs.org.uk/schoolgardening (Activities associated with nature but with a focus on plants and food production).

Equipment suppliers

Forest School Shop: http://forestschoolshop.co.uk

Greenman Bushcraft: http://greenmanbushcraft.co.uk

Mindstretchers: http://www.mindstretchers.co.uk/

Muddy Faces: www.muddyfaces.co.uk

Raindrops: http://www.raindrops.co.uk/ (Supplier of waterproof clothing for children and adults).

Viking Kids: http://www.vikingkids.co.uk/ (Supplier of waterproof clothing for children and adults).

Wildwood Bushcraft: http://www.wildwoodbushcraft.com/forest_school.htm

Networking and advice

Council for Learning Outside the Classroom: http://www.lotc.org.uk (Resources, Forest Education Network (FEN) and FEN Bulletins. The FEN is the successor body to the Forest Education Initiative (FEI) in England).

Institute for Outdoor Learning: http://www.outdoor-learning.org/ (Forest School Special Interest Group).

Geographical Association: http://www.geography.org.uk/ (Early Years and Primary resources).

Further resources

Training

Archimedes Training: http://www.forestschools.com/

Bridgwater College: http://www.bridgwater.ac.uk/subject.php?sector=6&subject=223

Bishops Wood: http://www.worcestershire.gov.uk/cms/bishops-wood-centre.aspx

Derbyshire County Council Forest Schools: http://www.derbyshire.gov.uk/education/schools_colleges/environmental_studies_service/forest_schools/default.asp

Eastwood Nursery School:www.urbanforestschool.co.uk (Introductory workshops, INSETS and consultancy services. Specialised in delivering Forest School in urban areas).

Forest Schools Birmingham: http://forestschoolsbirmingham.com/

Forest School Learning Initiative (Gloucestershire): http://www.forestschoollearning.co.uk/

Greenlight Trust: http://www.greenlighttrust.org/forest-schools/

Learning through Landscapes: www.ltl.org.uk (Short courses, consultancy services and reference materials on outdoor play and learning).

Lincolnshire Forest Schools: http://www.lincolnshireforestschools.co.uk/FAQ.aspx

Mindstretchers: http://www.mindstretchers.co.uk/ (Courses, consultancy services on nature kindergartens and Forest Schools).

Norfolk Forest Schools: http://www.schools.norfolk.gov.uk/Teaching-and-learning/Environmental-and-outdoor-learning/Forest-school/index.htm

Shropshire Council Forest School http://www.shropshire.gov.uk/schools.nsf/open/E800819EC9B43A67802575450054B50C

Sussex Wildlife Trust: http://www.sussexwildlifetrust.org.uk

Warwickshire Wildlife Trust: http://www.warwickshire-wildlife-trust.org.uk/about-forest-schools

Widehorizons Outdoor Education Trust (Greenwich): http://www.widehorizons.org.uk (Training and events).

Worcestershire County Council Forest Schools: http://www.worcestershire.gov.uk/cms/forest-schools.aspx

International websites

Children and Nature Network: http://www.childrenandnature.org/ (Information, links to international research and resources.)

Science Kids: http://www.sciencekids.co.nz/nature.html (Activities and resources on nature).

The Environmental Learning Network: www.naturenet.com/kidsthingstodooutside.htm (Ideas for fun and easy things children can do, educational resources, family resources and books for adults).

TLC Family: http://tlc.howstuffworks.com/family/nature-crafts.htm (Nature activities and projects).

Videos on Forest School

Conducting web searches on the topic 'Forest School video' will bring up options for you to preview. Videos can be useful in showing colleagues and parents the types of experiences Forest School fosters. Here are videos we found on YouTube and Teachers Media:

Charlbury School, Oxfordshire: http://www.teachersmedia.co.uk/videos/ks1-outdoor-learning-with-forest-school

Further resources

Dudley School: http://www.youtube.com/watch?v=Kk-3mPyNMcl&feature=related

Edwalton Primary School, Nottinghamshire: http://www.teachersmedia.co.uk/videos/ks1-ks2-geography-journey-sticks

Forest Schools Early Years: http://www.youtube.com/watch?v=bAR_OTMxNOs&feature=related

Highters Heath Primary School, inner city Birmingham: www.teachersmedia.co.uk/videos/inner-city-forest

Lanarkshire, Scotland: http://www.youtube.com/watch?v=g8WWrRzf7ZU&feature=related

MindStretchers Forest School: http://www.youtube.com/watch?v=ceLqvwxDdjk&feature=related

Neroche Forest Schools: http://www.youtube.com/watch?v=o8sj1HrZ7Nk&feature=related

Urban Forest School Eastwood Nursery in London, England: http://www.youtube.com/user/forestschoolmedia

Acknowledgements

Jenny Doyle

I would like to thank my family for their continued patience and support. Also my good friends Sheila Sage and Sue Durant for having faith and commitment to Forest School.

Katherine Milchem

I would like to thank my parents for instilling my love and curiosity for the natural world. Also thank you to headteacher Liz Rook for all her support throughout my career.

The authors would both like to thank the staff and parents in all the Forest School settings featured in this book, for permission to use the photos and case studies.

All images © MA Education Ltd. except pages 54, 60, 62, 64, 85 photos © Cath Mukhopadhyay. All other photos taken by Lucie Carlier apart from pages 2, 3, 6, 7, 10, 13, 14, 16, 18, 19, 22, 26, 27, 79, 80, 83, 98 photos taken by Jenny Doyle; pages 41, 43, 52, 59, 61, 65, 69, 81, 84, photos taken by Katherine Milchem.